PRAISE FOR *THE BUSINESS OF YOUR LIFE*

"*The Business of Your Life* covers all the basics, and *well*."

—**Christopher Farrell,**
Economics commentator,
Minnesota Public Radio,
Senior economics contributor, *Marketplace*.
Author of *Unretirement* and *The New Frugality*.

"A comprehensive, accessible, and faith-filled guide to thinking clearly about the meaning of your money. *The Business of Your Life* offers a splendid introduction to economics and personal finance and is just the sort of book I wish my father had given me as a young man."

—**Dr. Ryan N. S. Topping,**
Vice-President and Academic Dean,
Newman Theological College, Edmonton,
and author of *The Case for Catholic Education*.

"*The Business of Your Life* not only summarized many of the important financial concepts I've learned over my career, but also taught me some new ones. My children will definitely have to read this book."

—**Chad Skally,**
President,
Skally's Tax Service, Inc.

"The gifted author's deep Christian faith and expansive financial knowledge find each other in this inspirational work. This mission of blending the head and heart is also a refresher for educators."

—Fr. Scott Donahue,
President/CEO of Mercy Home
for Boys and Girls.

THE BUSINESS

of

YOUR LIFE

A Young Christian's Guide to
FINANCIAL LITERACY

Keith Lloyd Brown

The Business of Your Life: A Young Christian's Guide to Financial Literacy
© 2018 by Keith Lloyd Brown

Published by Deep River Books
Sisters, Oregon
www.deepriverbooks.com

Printed in the United States of America

ISBN – 13: 9781632695017
LOC: 2019930765

Cover Design by Joe Bailen

Printed in the USA

2018—First Edition
27 26 25 24 23 22 21 20 19 18   10 9 8 7 6 5 4 3 2 1

DEDICATION

I dedicate this work to young Christian men and women who, through no fault of their own, aren't given the loving attention and instruction on how to draw up a financial battle plan that empowers them to survive and prosper in the secular world.

Table of Contents

Table of Contents

ACKNOWLEDGMENTS

I'm glad I persevered in writing to you about personal finance. After all those invisible taps on the shoulder during my years as a financial planner, I was finally convinced that this is what God wanted me to do.

Many good people helped me get my intentions in print. Pastor Louis Montelongo clued me in that those of you in the homeschool sector would really appreciate a Christ-centered, personal-finance book, and Ms. Kelly Mack made me realize that curriculum directors at faith-based academies can't find much on the topic in the first place. I thank brother Bill for his help with my digital images; sister Barb—an applied student of the book arts; plus the rest of my family and friends for their support. And thanks to Mother, who was always supportive, I inherited a wry sense of humor. I'm grateful to Sally E. Stuart, Christian author and teacher, who patiently helped me stay on track; and I tip my hat to Marilyn Anderson for her expertise during my initial copyedit. Appreciation also has to go to Roger Reistad, Nick Vargo, Chad Skally and staff, the folks at Deluxe Check, and the city officials of Champaign, Illinois. Finally, my heartfelt gratitude goes out to those who reviewed my manuscript and offered suggestions and endorsements.

But none of these experiences would have mattered if Bill, Nancie, and Andy Carmichael of Deep River Books hadn't believed that you would actually read the coming chapters. Blessings to them and their staff, in particular Alexis Miller and Tamara Barnet, who deftly guided me through publication. Carl Simmons edited my work and Amit Dey and team typeset it beautifully. Thank You!

Chapter 1

What's All the Fuss?

Once again, the chatter was about people who "can't seem to get their financial act together." This time it was in a Dunkin' Donuts, instead of in a radio segment.

"Heck. Personal finanth is juth common thenth."

I wanted to tell the stranger not to talk with his mouth full, and not to couple personal finance with common sense. Having common sense isn't the answer (which is fortunate because some people don't seem to possess it). The fault occurs when a reasoned person attempts to apply a concrete discipline—such as mathematics—to the elusive concept of financial literacy. Consequently, the results are haphazard.

To successfully solve a problem of any type, you have to first know what you're working with. Looking for a definition of financial literacy in Merriam-Webster will prove fruitless, in this case; it doesn't exist there. Rather, financial knowhow is scattered throughout books on economics, law, taxes, insurance, accounting, and securities. Knowledge also shows up in fragments within periodicals, newspaper columns, TV programs, and on Internet sites. It's no wonder even college grads have trouble making "thenth" of it all.

So, let's start with a workable definition: Financial literacy is an acquired skill set, comprised of basic knowledge in key areas and an assortment of tools designed for a specific end purpose. Instead of wringing their hands, complainers and educators should just give you this complete set of tools and demonstrate how to accomplish that specific end purpose.

"What exactly *is* this specific end purpose?" I hear you ask. It's to make your business operation run profitably.

"What are you talking about, mister? I don't own a business!"

You most certainly do. You earn money, spend it, and hope to have some left over. You're running the "business of your life," and cannot afford to fail. As Chief Executive Officer (CEO) your objective is to move in the opposite direction of poverty.

The stark reality of occupied cardboard boxes under interstate bridges leads us to believe that some people are trying to run their business without a complete skill set. I don't want that to accidently happen to you, even though I'm sure you've been handling money pretty well since age ten. So, what's next?

Next are the intense challenges arising from increased income and higher expenses. My strategy to help you conquer them is to supplement what you're currently learning in school, and to fortify the skills you have under your belt. As we tackle the chapters ahead, you'll learn both practical applications and aspects of personal finance that aren't a standard part of contemporary curriculum. As I demonstrate tools and share industry secrets, be assured that you'll gain every skill and bit of knowledge you'll need to successfully manage your business.

Each chapter is designed to lead to financial independence—thereby bolstering your ability to build an equitable society, respond to appeals, and responsibly care for our planet as you do for yourself. The book ends with a picture of what happens if you crash the bus.

Key terms to know are presented in boldfaced type, **like this**, and I strive to define them within their given paragraphs. With a wicked vocabulary, you'll be able to drop *debenture, derivative,* and *fiduciary* in front of your folks. These terms also comprise the index, which serves as a trail marker now and for the years to come.

To enrich your understanding of a new financial word or topic, I recommend investopedia.com. But any word search, as you know, will produce a ton of information. In that respect the Web has become immensely helpful. Digging there also brings up opinion blogs, retailers, and distributors of financial products. I say that as a reminder, because it's easy to forget that people and institutions position themselves there to make money.

At the end of each chapter I've listed URLs for referenced concepts, topics, and supplementary sources. For example, our nation's executive branch offers www.mymoney.gov; and the American Institute of Certified Public Accountants (AICPA) reinforces what you'll learn here by visiting their website, www.360financialliteracy.org. These professionals have been hammering millennials with billboards lately to get them to save.

What you won't find ahead are schemes to amass the equivalent of a king's ransom. An obsession with money is just another obsession to lead you off course. If future blessings do include a sizable accumulation of wealth, you'll have the resources necessary to someday craft an endowment, trust, or foundation—all of which will aid others long after you're six feet under. And an estate-planning attorney will help you pass wealth to others with minimal tax consequences. The world half-jokingly says, "You can't take it with you," which is hardly sage advice compared with the expectation that you're not going to need it anyhow.

You won't find unsolicited advice ahead, either. Our Creator didn't wire our brains with reception antennae, but human behavior suggests that He left a few connections open to inquisitiveness and self-thinking, once we've absorbed knowledge and truth. This blessing allows us to think and live uniquely, rather than being automatons.

You will find ahead, by the way, chapter-and-verse-only Scripture notations. In that way you can use the Bible of your choice to reference them.

Becoming financially independent is not the same as becoming independently wealthy. Just as cold is the absence of heat, I define "financial independence" as an absence of financial insecurities. One example is running out of paycheck before running out of month. Another is having the bank dishonor your check. While both events are painful, the real threat to a happy life is accumulating so many financial insecurities that, in total, they ultimately destabilize your marriage—if that union is what God has planned for you.

In managing your earnings to accomplish your objectives, I suggest you imitate Michelangelo and be creative with knowledge you gain here. When all is said and done, personal finance is really more of an art than any of the sciences, which have no room for expression or multiple answers. The degree of financial literacy you ultimately reach will determine how close you'll get to the masterpiece you first had in mind.

Moreover, this skill set adds to a healthy mental outlook—which can be less resilient than the outlook of your heart. Hearts mend in due time. Moms are right when saying, "There are other fish in the sea." Conversely, the blues won't let go when you can't make the rent each month. You know exactly from experience what makes the clouds evaporate: mastering a skill, or completing a difficult project, justifiably makes you beam with pride and stokes your self-confidence.

As in your spiritual journey, you need sharp skills in the marketplace to defend yourself against people who operate from a position of unfair advantage. Competing with honest men and women is tough enough without having to watch for sharks—like **predatory lenders**, who take financial advantage of uninformed people or those in immediate need. The range of practice is wide, including burdensome payday loans, mortgages with poor terms, and various manipulative business practices. Search "predatory lending" to find more examples.

Many such arrangements are deemed usurious. **Usury**, which is now defined as the practice of charging an interest rate that's far higher than the going rate, was first known as the cost of using someone else's money. The non-bank lenders above—including pawnbrokers—fall within the **subprime lending market**. You're forced to borrow here when you have a low credit score and minimal assets. The subprime is a subset of the larger **secondary lending market**, which represents varied alternatives. For example, if your folks lend you the money to buy a car, they are part of the secondary market. The **prime lending market** includes state and federally regulated banks, thrifts, and credit unions.

This less-than-desirable subprime market won't go away, despite humane society's best efforts to lend a hand to those who find themselves subject to it. There are just too many people who are unwilling or unable by circumstance to get their act together. In its defense, the subprime does serve a community need. Upright business owners, who have been at the bottom themselves, are there to serve the undereducated and disadvantaged—but shouldn't work them over. As the Lord tells us, the poor will always be with us (Matt. 26:11). But I doubt that this was simple commentary, since He didn't engage in small talk. Rather, He envisioned our inadequacies. Yes, poverty in its many forms can be circumstantial, but Jesus calls us all to do better, regardless of our state in life, as He does in the parable of the bags of gold—as some translations state it (Matt. 25:14–30).

Some municipalities have explored banning operators they view as undesirable, but doing so may be constitutionally impossible, and outlawing them will only create a larger, less regulated black market. As it is, state and local governments follow a zigzag pattern of regulating these businesses and educating the public. An effective way to deal with the issue is to create effective usury legislation that puts a floating cap on this market's interest rates. Ideally, the law's maximum should rise and fall relative to the **prime rate**. If you recall from economics, the prime rate is what traditional banks and credit unions charge their best customers. Moreover, we must do what we can to help the less fortunate move upward.

On a national level, during the early part of this century, our country experienced the symptoms of predatory lending, due in part to the avalanche of mortgage-loan defaults. The details of this long story are best discussed in a different book, but it's important to emphasize that some financial operators intentionally packaged "garbage mortgages" and sold them as singular cuts of prime beef, making that sin one of the fundamental causes of distress. A search on the Web for "predatory lending and mortgage default crisis" will bring up plenty of stories.

Our faith isn't opposed to lending with interest *per se*. Our belief set takes into account that the money necessary to build homes, office buildings, churches, roads, and dams can't come solely from profits, donations, and taxes. To erect the walls, we need to compensate investors for lending their savings—which they've put at risk of loss in the process.

Lending with interest at a personal level is quite another thing. Our faith maintains that if you front me some money, you should not ask for more in return. That practice leaves me worse off than I was. We find references in the Bible to this as far back as Ezekiel 18:8.

Reflecting on interpersonal lending is relevant, as you develop your own personal philosophy: If I ask you for a loan to meet a necessity, you must rightfully consider first if my request fits into your budget. If you think it does and you lend interest-free, we're both in luck—an act of mercy like that is a beautiful treasure to lay up in heaven. If the repayment date passes and the specter of loss gnaws at you, then either you actually couldn't afford to lend me the money in the first place, or you have a quite strong attachment to the stuff. To avoid having the matter become a point of contention when your own assets are limited, it may be better to turn me down in self-defense. That would not be uncharitable. If I ask for a loan to buy a luxury, your internal discourse won't be much different, but in this case it's much easier to respond flatly with "no." After all, are you really in the lending business? TV episodes of *Judge Judy* suggest otherwise.

In time, you may choose to make **charitable giving** a permanent part of your budget. Then you have the option to say, "Just keep the money." In reality, if I can't afford a necessity right now, what reason do you have to believe that I will anytime soon? Our Jewish friends carved out eight insightful levels of charitable giving; check them out in the link at the end of this chapter.

Department stores and the like strive to make *your* budget go to *their* business. The goal of raw **capitalism** is not to keep you fed and in fashion—it's to move money from designer-jean pockets into armored trucks. In the war to win sales, retailers and service providers launch intense advertising bombardments that assault the will. To make matters worse, Madison Avenue's slick marketing insults the intelligence.

All systems of trade are the indispensable engines that drive economies, but those that overheat cause inflation; consume valuable resources; and, among other things, damage global cultures and clash with religions. These circumstances have become politically hot topics around the world, especially since digital commerce began. Such is **consumerism**.

Not surprisingly, there's resistance to it. People who adhere to the "simple living" lifestyle express their philosophy and ideas through art, literature, popular culture, politics, and religion. Some are activists in the green movement, while others stand steady by living, working, and playing passively. Two good Christian examples are the Amish and the Religious Society of Friends (Quakers). Search the Web to learn more about "simple living."

Despite their political differences, Republican and Democrat business owners agree that an effective way for people to raise their economic and social status is by joining the club. Either you'll create a company based on the three basic business structures featured in Chapter 8 of this book, or you'll work for one—unless you plan to be a professional student. Owning an enterprise may not be your cup of tea, but you should and can own part of one or more companies by at least becoming a passive investor—which I'll show you how to do.

Before we wade into that pond, imagine that your teacher jotted a list of basic financial skills on the board:

1. Demonstrate how you make your checkbook balance agree with your bank statement.

2. Name an investment that simultaneously reduces taxes and builds wealth.

3. Tell the class how you create a budget and track its performance.

4. Describe your filing system.

5. Explain what actually happens in bankruptcy.

6. Enlighten others about the difference between a stock and a bond.

7. What's the philosophy behind a defined contribution plan?

8. When do you have to file your first tax return?

9. How much life insurance should you buy?

10. If you lose your checkbook, what steps are necessary to protect yourself?

How many of her examples could you confidently tackle to impress your classmates? If you feel shaky trying to answer some or all of these requests, charitably remind yourself that if you had the chalk in your hand and an apple on your desk, you wouldn't have picked up this book in the first place—but you'll be able to by the time you're finished. If you can already answer the majority of what's on the board, patiently bear in mind that, for the sake of those who haven't had your experience, I can't filter out what you already know. (Nor will I lose any sleep over you.) Move past the topic if you're sure you've mastered it.

I did include some content that isn't essential right now. When we reach these few points I'll let you know, and you can skip down if you don't find them important. But in the interest of completeness, I won't cheat anyone out of the chance to learn about them.

Remember, this book is a guide—not an end in itself, and you're rapidly approaching the point in your life where uncovering knowledge and truth is going to be left up to you. After you return your rented cap and gown, no one else is going to make the effort to gather financial knowledge and skills into one place for you, as I have, nor will anyone take the time to study it with you.

I wish you every success in running the business of your life.

Helpful Links

Federal Trade Commission

https://www.ftc.gov

U.S. Department of the Treasury

https://www.treasury.gov/resource-center/financial-education/
Documents/National%20Strategy%202016%20Update.pdf

https://www.treasury.gov/resource-center/financial-education/
Documents/College%20Savings%20and%20Financing%20
Resources%20FLEC%202016.pdf

Executive branch

https://www.mymoney.gov/Pages/default.aspx

American Institute of Certified Public Accountants

https://www.360financialliteracy.org/

Eight levels of charitable giving

http://www.jewishvirtuallibrary.org/eight-levels-of-charitable-giving

Chapter 2

WHY DO WE NEED MONEY?

If you've ever asked questions like, "Mom, why can't we go to the store and get what we want without paying?" and "Why can't everything be free?" you might have heard back, "Be serious, child." If you did, then you asked someone who never really gave the matter a second thought.

These are actually fair questions, and deep ones at that. Kids are paying close attention during the process of figuring out how to get through life, and invariably ask similar ones. It's not just idle curiosity. The notion of money becomes a disturbance, and they're searching for answers that make sense. Up until then, they took money for granted. Their contemplation progresses from, "Why can't you just write a check?" to wondering why the earth and sea's abundance isn't a free inheritance. They scratch their heads as to why the whole world can't operate like a giant family.

Just when does this transformative thinking about the nature of money begin? In child development, the age of seven is widely accepted as a benchmark for the gift of reason to emerge. Children at that age start understanding why right is right and wrong is wrong—what's natural and what's not. The process of rational thinking is under way.

But regarding money, this window in time doesn't seem to stay open long. When certain parents, guardians, or teachers give trusting youngsters the impression that currency's reason for existence should be self-evident and that more on the subject is extraneous, kids tend to let the subject drop. So, should the topic be left unexplored? Our chapter title implies otherwise. By gaining some perspective on the nature of money and examining its root causes, this insight may leave you less likely to be taken advantage of—which is an important goal of this book.

If you raise that window enough to step through, you'll find confirmation in the first chapters of Genesis of what the kids had first suspected. Part of God's eternal plan had been to freely give Adam and Eve, whom He had placed in paradise to work as caretakers (Gen. 2:15), all the bounty of His creation (Gen. 1:29), plus the authority to manage the world (Gen. 1:28). With the exception of one tree (Gen. 2:17), no strings were attached. There was no ATM—all truly was free.

What changed everything, of course, was that act of disobedience. Adam and Eve had trusted in the lies of the serpent and disregarded the Creator's command. God banished humankind from the garden and set us at task to accomplish survival through blood, sweat, and tears (Gen 3:17–19). With these additional elements, the definition of what it means to work expanded from what should have been the joyous odyssey of furthering creation to an arduous journey with no relief in sight. Only thousands of years later did He send our Savior.

According to Scripture, innovative descendants of our first parents had already begun the practice of trading something of agreed value for alternate needs and wants. In Genesis 17:27, a reference to Abraham's "bought servants" indicates that a solution was afoot to a problem common to societies. Historians, anthropologists, and economists are not in complete agreement about when or why a monetary system evolved. That probably has less to do with an inability to synthesize theories and more to do with the fact that ancient history doesn't tell us everything. Artifacts and sketchy information are all that researchers have as clues. Evidence suggests that the earliest coins date back to 2700 BC in what's now Turkey; and older round, engraved metal disks with square piercings were found in China—suggesting a string of money. For millennia, apparently objects that aren't easily counterfeited have served as testaments to society's fight against corruption.

A strong developmental theory is that money came about from its usefulness. The ancients could then exchange this object of agreed value for that warm goatskin, instead of the two chickens and loaf of bread they carried under their arms. Without money today, how much junk do you think you'd have to drag to a BMW dealership? Slick as it is, currency hasn't entirely replaced bartering. It still coexists with monetary systems in world economies.

Gold fever—our obsession with what seems precious—fits into the puzzle, as well. But our desire to possess beauty in the hand would wait patiently for Mister Ingenuity to marry Miss Intrigued. Once upon a time, that happened. Early daredevils realized that when they got the fire hot enough, they could melt rock just like the volcanoes, and later figured out how to separate out the curious part before the hell-like liquid cooled. Those who would become the "smiths" forged this brainchild into iron swords and plows. Well, it was a short leap from there into the Bronze Age and, within no time, graduates of Manufacturing 101 were producing brilliant gold and silver art forms to adorn bodies. Striking coins was just down the street. Progress had set the stage for any civilized group of tribes that coalesced into a nation to blend the usefulness theory, the human dynamic of obsession, and our instinctual need for uniformity into an institutional system of trade. With precious metals accepted as the universal medium of exchange, their circulation occasioned the world's first effective distribution of wealth.

Central to an economy's success are prescribed standards of weight and measure, like pounds, gallons, and meters. They're there for comparative value and for ensuring that everyone plays by the same rules. An early example of weight is the shekel, which originally may have been an agreed number of uniformly sized grains that fit into two hands— presumably enough for a dinner loaf. And, apparently, the Hebrews converted the shekel's weight into a silver coin. All self-imposed standards and rules that govern trade possess the virtuous and purposeful effect of instilling confidence, trust, and harmony in the marketplace. Creating this atmosphere is a shining example of humankind's revered side. Negativity, like the thumb's pressure on a scale, is always to be cast off because it assails Hope—one of the "Big Three" (1 Cor. 13:13). And the idiom that "there is honor among thieves" makes you realize that even the troublemakers wave this flag.

If you really get into causal theories about how money impacted the way societies evolved, and want to learn about how modern economies function, you'll rightly find more on the economics shelf. Volumes there span the ideas of both classic and contemporary economists. Adam Smith's *The Wealth of Nations* is not light reading—nor, for that matter, are the writings of John Maynard Keynes and John Kenneth Galbraith—but they are rewarding reads.

Before you can arrive at a complete understanding about money, you need to include the unflattering aspects of our fallen nature. To a person, we're imperfect beings, to say the least. Why else would the place where you store your stuff at school to be called a "lock-er"? Vice, in its many forms, is generally not included in the secular world's reasoning about why we're stuck with money, yet it has to be another piece of the puzzle because it was conceived in the mind and fashioned by the hand of a creature in struggle.

To dramatize how rebellious behavior fits into the picture, I use the instrument that authors of films, novels, and plays do to communicate a point: They tell a story, whether real-life or fictional.

Thus, our little tale of conflict and resolution opens with leaders of long, long ago sitting around a campfire at their tribal-council meeting. Some were worked up, and turned to the elder for help in managing their crews:

"Chief! You've got to help us do something about guys who constantly lie about being sick. They want to stay in bed, instead of working the fields or chopping down trees. Others at the quarry spend most of the day taking breaks."

Before the foreman could finish, a head honcho interjected, "Ditto! I've got shepherds who sneak off in the heat of the day."

Then, in a chorus of discontent, they all complained, "The bums show up at night, demanding to be fed with the rest of the crew!"

"Kicking them out doesn't solve anything," voiced another. "The losers just move to another village, and we unwittingly take in *their* lazy outcasts to replace them. You can't tell the good from the bad by looking at them. The only marked man we know of was Cain."

"And what about the lion hunters, who think we can't survive without their intrepid bravery? One bunch demands special treatment or threatens to go on strike," warned another.

"Calm down, my friends. I have an idea," soothed the elder. "At the end of the day, write a note for all workers who have pulled their weight and have them present it to the cook. Those without, go without." (The Apostles to the Nations echoed that sentiment in 2 Thess. 3:10.)

"But I can't write, and my cook can't read!" lamented a boss.

"Better yet," replied the wise chief, "take smooth, small, flat stones from the Tigris or Euphrates, and have your talented one [like Tubal-Cain in Genesis 4:22] carve a unique design—using it as your tribal symbol. You can distribute those instead of notes, and reward your hardest workers and the high-value crew with a few extra, if need be. They can trade these tokens with Bill Butcher for warm animal skins, or with Barb Baker for hot bread. Bill and Barb can exchange the rocks with Smitty for keener knives and bigger ovens—and so on. Before you know it, the whole village will get into the act, and your problems will be solved."

I'll conclude this corny tale here, even though you know the chief was only partially right. But is this really the way money was invented? I can't offer any proof, nor do I assert that it is. Yet, is this portrayal wholly without basis? Certainly, this script will never make it to Broadway but before anyone dismisses it with the fairy-tale belief that primal family ties didn't have knots and that village relationships were always rosy, the doubter needs to recall some facts: By this time, Cain had already killed his own brother. Second, the Creator eventually became so grieved with the great wickedness of the men on earth that, by the sixth chapter of the first book, He was telling Noah to start building an ark. Considering the above, how would anybody think that less malevolent acts of deceit, laziness, and manipulation in the fictional account had never been perpetrated before or after the deluge?

We're not that far removed from the post-Neanderthals. We still use money to influence behavior and to approximate justice, which alone has its day in heaven. It is a most excellent invention.

What you think of an object influences how much respect you afford it. Reject any notion that money is bad. An inanimate object doesn't possess behavioral traits. Nor should people mistakenly believe that money is the root of all evil. Paul knew better, and wisely admonished us in 1 Timothy 6:10 that covetousness of money leads us astray.

Wages serve a dual purpose as well. Not only does a "handful" (or the swipe of a card) get you in the door—its mere possession becomes assumed proof to the ticket taker that you've met the work requirements to claim it. Your callouses and migraines are the badges of honor that prove you've come by your paycheck honestly—making any type of robbery doubly reprehensible.

And what of those work requirements? They're the two elephants in the room. One represents the fact that God mandated we labor, thereby conferring on us the inalienable right to do so (a social issue you'll bump up against). Pachyderm two represents our necessary interdependence as we struggle to survive on a sometimes hostile planet.

How well we pay one another is up to us (another cause to champion). Over the ages, we've used compensation to honor Him and glorify Him through magnificent achievements in music (i.e., J. S. Bach), agriculture, literature and art, architecture (such as the Cathedral of St. Paul

Photo by W. P. Brown, 2009

in Minnesota, shown above), and math and science—even to the degree that our fallen astronauts have "reached up," as President Reagan eulogized, "and touched the face of God."

As a lad of nine, I heard that Baptists, whom I knew nothing about at the time, weren't supposed to play cards. Yet, Dad's uncle Sam married one, and Aunt Lill loved playing "five hundred" with the family, as well as other card games. *What's up with that?* I wondered. Years later, I realized that poker games with monetary stakes were the issue. The Southern Baptist Convention adopted its "Resolution on Gambling" when it met in Kansas City, Missouri in 1984. In reading, you'll quickly understand the reasons Baptists believe institutionalized gambling is detrimental to families and to the nation. The Church of Jesus Christ of Latter-day Saints is morally opposed to gambling and lotteries as well. Additionally, the Mormons have an expansive, comprehensive charity network, designed to meet immediate needs and to help people get back on their feet and lead productive lives. (Both statement links are at the end of this chapter.) The Church of Rome is less specific concerning gambling, but perhaps as importantly, Catholics have long been counseled to avoid the near-occasions of any sin—consistent with a nonliteral interpretation of Matthew 18:8–9.

An online search of how other denominations view money will tell you more. Avoid the opinions of bloggers, and search for the truth yourself in all matters—not just religion.

So, have the above arguments answered our original question of why everything isn't free? (How will you answer *your* kids someday?) Perhaps the practical reasons are academic. We'll have to accept things the way they are and get on with earning a living, and can do so with a better perspective on money. But that doesn't mean our children's disappointment isn't justified. It takes a child to suggest what the world would have been like if the devil hadn't swayed Adam and Eve. We'll all have to wait for act two—trusting in the Lord that we won't be left on the outside, looking in. The apostle Paul offers us hope of that brighter day (1 Cor. 2:9). We have no comprehension of what's in store.

Equally, kids must take into account that cultures formed from radically different points of view. Christopher Columbus didn't find a monetary system when he landed in the Americas, but he also didn't encounter a naval armada, ready to defend the homeland against an invasion. The native peoples hadn't been seafarers like those of, say, Europe and Scandinavia. They were tied, and continue to be inexorably tied, to mother earth.

Why the great differences within cultures and races on earth? We impatiently look to ourselves to explain them in the profound belief, which is rooted in having already discovered vast volumes of temporal knowledge, that we can find all answers simply through self-study and exploration. Smart as we are (or think we are), we won't discern how our differences fit into God's eternal plan for salvation until He reveals them in the time and manner of His choosing.

Helpful Links

Southern Baptist "Resolution on Gambling"

http://www.sbc.net/resolutions/564/resolution-on-gambling

Latter Day Saints position on gambling

https://www.lds.org/topics/gambling?lang=eng

Chapter 3

Being Your Own Secretary

With plenty to do before graduation, it's difficult to dedicate time to the two tasks of setting up your office and doing what's necessary to nail a work interview.

"Office? Do I need an actual office?" That would be ideal someday, but some semblance of one in your room now will help keep you organized, and should maximize your chances of getting hired. Since you can't afford to hire a secretary and a public relations agent, I'm here to help you to make quick work of your organizational tasks, and then focus your attention on the key preliminaries of landing employment. As you know all too well, gifts and allowances (either of them is a form of **subsidy**) don't go very far.

Documentation

Every company or institution you interact with wants probable assurance of getting what it wants before giving you what *you* want—which subjects you to their blank application. Whether one is for a job, consumer loan, or credit card, these examination-like worksheets demand current personal information, and may ask you to cite past addresses and employers—complete with dates, salary history, physical addresses, and supervisor names. If that isn't enough, you may be required to submit your complete educational history.

I used to dread filling out an application because it took so much effort and time to find the data. I was disorganized. You may be better at this than I was, and can ask your friends where *they* keep the information. Maybe it's memorized. Maybe it's in their phone or backed-up virtual file.

But where do they preserve valuable documents and cherished memorabilia? Most of us just cram our belongings in one place when we need to clean our rooms. Do you, yourself, store your important papers with socks? What's the record time it took for you to find something? Realizing how much stuff students have in their rooms makes suggesting a four-drawer, fireproof steel file cabinet a bit premature.

Champions have found that it's prudent to eventually rent a safe-deposit box to protect themselves from tornadoes, floods, and burglaries. It's a sanctuary for, say, expensive jewelry, bonds, marriage licenses, adoption papers, military discharge orders, etc. Do you have a certified copy of your birth certificate? You'll need one for a passport. Do you have your baptismal record? You'll need that one day, too. Here's their ideal place. Wills, trusts, and life insurance policies are protected there, as well.

Renters insurance has your back in the event of fire or theft, but it can't replicate one-of-a-kind documents. Their safest haven is your county Register of Deeds. This government servant will take responsibility for their perpetual retention, and gladly produce as many certified copies as you need—even fifty years from now.

Organization Essentials

To aid with the tasks of archiving and efficiently retrieving critical data, I offer you a cheap, small cabinet and a filing system to go along with it: the bankers box, available at any office-supply store. Its dimensions accommodate either letter or legal-size manila folders and expandable file jackets. (See Figure 3-1.) Expandable file jackets work well as large envelopes for records and receipts. Their pocket-like design precludes small items from slipping into no-man's-land, and the facing area of the back panel is designed for content identification. Artistic people mark the area by hand but, if you're like me, apply labels printed in your desired font and color. The heading examples shown in the illustration are a good start. Not by chance, a bankers box fits nicely on a closet shelf to keep your little brother's nose out and helps give your folks the appearance of a clean room. Best of all, you'll now know where to find what you're looking for.

Figure 3-1   Bankers Box

I dare say the most valuable file you'll create will have your own name on it, and be marked "Permanent." This brands it as a conservatory that you'll maintain forever. Drop in that list of residences and employment history. It's also the right place for your Social Security card, rather than your wallet or purse. If you're "smarter than the average bear," you'll request a transcript from every educational institution you attend and tuck it safely inside.

When you've filed your stack of loose papers in labeled jackets, you're prepared to knock out any application without having to fudge what you can't recall. This will help you sleep better, knowing that evaluators routinely cross-reference and verify data with what's on your credit report, and other inquiries they make.

Job Search Essentials

When you're able to present accurate data in an enhanced format at the drop of a hat, you move yourself up some twenty spaces in line. Applicants viewed as professionals in their field are the ones who land the jobs and promotions. What constitutes an enhanced format? Let's look at the different pieces.

The Résumé

A good portion of it is your **résumé**, which is a written expanded personal profile submitted with an employment application. As your own PR agent, use your English skills to give your image as professional a polish as some of you girls give to your nails. Design this glowing, yet truthful, document in a fashion that gives the human resources manager good reason to choose your application from among the dozens of others. **Résumé** templates are on the Web for the do-it-yourselfers, and many books are out there to help you write an excellent one.

The Cover Letter

The **cover letter** is a powerful tool that acts as an introduction to your application and allows you to toot your own horn. In this biographical attention-getter, share personal attributes that complement the advertised job openings—keeping in mind that "temperance in all things" applies here too. But you can certainly volunteer that you absolutely love sales, are mechanically inclined, learn quickly, are eager to please, have dependable transportation, or are on the honor roll. Many of you have volunteered for causes, delivered meals, and been involved with fundraisers for organized sports or band. Some of you can operate massive farm equipment with your eyes closed. This stuff counts most when your job history section seems to lack substance. Such traits and life experiences are valued by employers who don't, or can't, ask about them.

Other life experiences include scouting, the Troops of Saint George, FFA, 4-H, the Civil Air Patrol, JROTC, and Junior Achievement. Future leaders emerge from such organizations, and bonding experiences within them produce wholesome, lifelong friendships.

Organizational membership also does a number on loneliness, which is a cancer devouring Hope. Remaining in a wee world can lead to depression. Symptoms include "nobody likes me." Really? More probably, few people know who you really are and can appreciate you. Close Facebook and go perform a random act of kindness. Better yet, give up your seat on the bus to the boy who's picking on you. Or, on a sweltering day, give a bottle of water to that girl who's totally rude—and then walk away. (You probably have even better ideas.) Jesus calls us to do things like this anyway—even though they're difficult (see Luke 6:32–36).

Sample application cover letters are online, but don't assume that all are good. Read them from an employer's perspective and ask yourself if you would hire this person.

Personal References

In addition to a cover letter, a list of personal and professional references bolsters your image on applications. Courteously let former employers, coaches, pastors, teachers, and even neighbors know that you would appreciate their good word if called. These people truly care about you and want you to succeed. Skip your parents, who would be considered biased by a prospective employer.

Speaking of friends, a devoted secretary will remind you that in your job search, it's not always what you know, but whom you know, that can make a difference. In time, develop a network of professional and tradespeople for consultation about projects and issues. You will meet educated, influential individuals by joining such civic groups as the Lions Club, the Rotary Club, church committees, and volunteer organizations. The fact that you're a participant makes a difference to prospective employers, and it makes a difference to those who receive your kind help. Immerse yourself in causes that interest you, and doors will open when you least expect them.

Essential Reference Books

All of your hard work counts for nothing if your written English is poor, casting you as illiterate and causing your correspondence to be promptly recycled. If you're working from a word processing program, your first line of defense is the grammar and spellcheck feature, but don't depend on it solely.

Three reference books are your refuge—especially for term papers, which shouldn't be written in the conversational style of this book. *The Chicago Manual of Style* can serve as the grammar teacher you'll be leaving behind. If your budget doesn't allow for a copy that's hot off the press, check for a used one on eBay. (For one buck, I recently picked up a handsome replacement.) The same can be said for a comprehensive dictionary, despite the fact that you can easily look up words online. Lastly is some version of *Roget's Thesaurus*, because if you ever hope to communicate well with the ones you love—as well as with friends and associates—you'll need to find the words to express yourself. This learning process is made easier by exploring a hard copy, which graphically shows how Roget outlined the English language. You'll find your words within his following eight classes, which, in total, remind us that humankind doesn't exist in a vacuum but is woven into God's world:

1. Abstract Relations
2. Space
3. Physics
4. Matter

5. Sensation
6. Intellect
7. Volition
8. Affections

Job Search Ideas

Consider applying with a "temp" agency if you're trying to squeeze into the job market. It can often be a path of least resistance. For example, when I supervised a maintenance department, I hired several great people from the pool of temps sent over to complete my special projects. That tactic was more fruitful than throwing a dart at faceless applications.

Clerical temp agencies are always looking for individuals with fast, efficient keyboarding skills, along with a good knowledge of the Microsoft Office suite. This could be a route for you because, if you didn't know, agency clients routinely offer full-time status to well-qualified temps. But you not only have to be proficient in software; your English has to be impeccable.

If you're online, Office software connects you to tutorials on Word, Excel, PowerPoint, and Outlook, and software reference books help when you aren't online. Used editions on eBay are affordable, and you're likely to find copies at the library. These volumes let you work at your own pace and discretion, and the training they afford is extraordinary.

When you're called for an interview, dress smartly and be well-groomed—employers want quality people, just as you seek to make high-caliber friends. Try to relax and be confident. At your age, you're not expected to know how to put a man on the moon. With entry-level jobs, employers are primarily looking for willing workers with a good attitude who can get along with others. Training will come—in the meantime, employers are more interested in having you show up on time with a clean smiling face. For tips on sharpening interviewing skills, search on the term "interview," and take in the results.

Military service after high school might fit you, as well. You can learn skills, develop lifelong friendships, and enjoy the benefits of the GI Bill afterward. Besides the infantry, there are hundreds of job classifications. Although Thomas Edison knocked out the candlestick-makers, the armed forces still need butchers and bakers, along with accountants, military-band members, payroll clerks, and communications specialists. The sharpest recruits are invited to attend officer candidate school (OCS). Both enlisted personnel and officers are required to advance by meeting higher educational and skill standards—along with maintaining physical fitness. Those who can't cut it receive discharge orders.

If physical safety in the Army, Navy, or Air Force concerns you, weigh their mortality statistics against the forty thousand or so souls who are killed on American roads each year—not to mention the countless injured or disabled ones (see the links at the end of this chapter).

Learning More about Yourself

Your work-search results will also improve if you know more about how you relate to the world and how it relates to you, just as med-school students before you have gone to school for the express purpose of telling you how your deviation from the body's ideal chemical makeup makes you feel and act differently from others. (You would think by now that doctors could come up with a gentler word than "disease" to classify such variations.) Several external evaluators can help with the former. The IQ (intelligence quotient) and Wechsler Adult Intelligence Scale (WAIS) tests are among those listed at the end of this chapter. The others will give you a broader exposure if you want to learn about what else is available. (Keep in mind that any "free IQ tests" you come across while searching online are being offered by companies that want to do business with you.)

You can raise your IQ score through quality arts education—especially with regard to the verbal tests. As you encounter more life experiences and study the sciences, you obtain a better picture of how God has interconnected all aspects of the world, which helps raise your performance-test results.

Another type of evaluator is the personality test. The most widely recognized one is the **Myers-Briggs Type Indicator** (MBTI), which offers an amazing insight into your personality type. A qualified professional interprets your personal-traits inventory, and places you within a sixteen-block table of different personality types. The report will:

- Describe your type characteristics,
- Showcase your strengths and unique gifts,
- Tell you how others may see you, and
- Comment about areas of potential growth.

It's much more fun and justly rewarding to take the test as a group. Employers implement the MBTI to enhance team performance. Knowing more about one another's personalities, likes, and dislikes raises the probability that personal interaction will be more understanding and productive. Type awareness certainly helps you develop friendships. In fact, it may help with a courtship, if each party ran through the program and compared notes.

Close relatives of the MBTI are vocational-guidance tests. One I took ranked me at the top for an airline pilot, but pegged me as a so-so editorial worker. I also topped the charts on securities and investment aptitude, but it ranked me low as a high school teacher and near the bottom as a university professor. That rang true, considering I am averse to teaching multiple personalities face-to-face. (Anyone with the same MBTI type knows this about me.) My introversion caused me to write a book instead of becoming a teacher like Sister Alice Gertrude (a real person) or Severus Snape of Hogwarts.

It's fascinating to know more things about yourself. In fact, no one is more interested in you than you are. You might already be exploring such resources on your tablet. Tests can be coordinated with parents or guardians and are administered by licensed professionals trained to interpret them. All three will inspire self-confidence when the results come back—owing to their glimpse into the towering strengths and hidden talents that God has given you. He created you uniquely and loves you profoundly.

Common sense has a place as well. You shouldn't take various program feedback lightly, nor take it too seriously. Their greatest value is an insight into who you are—not a measure of it.

In review: Get yourself organized and learn more about yourself, and then communicate your skills to the world with impeccable English and diction. Who wants to still be washing dishes in their thirties?

But wait, there's more. If you want to command a higher salary, then position yourself past ordinary school. Become refined. Though it's been more than sixty years since finishing schools have prepared young women for entry into society (mostly because society has changed), both young men and women still benefit from admirable deportment, knowing proper etiquette, and by learning social graces. The fact that *Amy Vanderbilt's Complete Book of Etiquette* is in its 50th Anniversary Edition is testament to the content's perpetual value. Amazon sellers have various copies for as little as ten dollars.

Helpful Links

Intelligence Tests
Weschler Adult Intelligence Scale:
https://wechslertest.com/

Cattell Culture Fair III
Search "Cattell IQ Test" for links and description.

Differential Ability Scales II
https://en.wikipedia.org/wiki/Differential_Ability_Scales
Search "Differential Ability Scales" for description and scholarly articles.

Stanford-Binet Intelligence Scales

https://stanfordbinettest.com

Woodcock-Johnson Tests of Cognitive Ability

https://www.hmhco.com/programs/woodcock-johnson-iv

Personality Tests

MBTI

http://www.myersbriggs.org/my-mbti-personality-type/mbti-basics

Facts about Military and Traffic Mortalities

https://www.va.gov/opa/publications/factsheets/fs_americas_wars.pdf

https://www.nytimes.com/2017/02/15/business/highway-traffic-safety.html

Chapter 4

THE ELEMENTS OF BANKING

Decisions frequently revolve around the age-old questions of who, what, when, where, why, and how:

"Who am I going with to homecoming?"

"What am I going to wear?"

"When is he picking me up?"

"Where are my shoes?"

"Oh, yeah. Why am I going with him in the first place?"

And, finally, "How do I look?"

Do these questions suggest that girls aren't quick to decide? No, not by definition. They should remind you that the female genius is relationship-oriented. Boys ask a lot of questions, too, but not aloud— or for directions. The male genius makes him look under rocks. When it comes to choosing which bank to dance with, good-natured kidding and emotions should drop out of the equation, yet these important pronouns and adverbs still deserve attention:

"Does this bank enjoy a good reputation?"

"Do its products and services meet my objectives?"

"Is this the time to begin a banking relationship?"

"Does it have convenient branches, irrespective of online access?"

"Why am I staying with this starter bank, where my folks and I opened a joint account?"

And, lastly, "How well am I now positioned to run the business of my life?"

Chances of getting what you want improve when you have respectable deposits in a place where officers and tellers know who you are—assuming you have a good credit score. (Chapter 13, on bankruptcy, covers credit reports as well as how to receive your free copy.) As with all relationships, it's best to know as much as you can about the other party. To that end, we'll cover bank types, rules, products, services, and account types, in the interest of making your banking experience pleasant and trouble-free.

Banking Overview

Functionally, banks accept the checking and savings deposits of families and companies and make them available for consumer loans, business loans, and home financing. That makes bankers middlemen—who rightfully deserve to be paid. Bank income is partially derived from charging an interest rate that's higher on loans than what it pays on deposits. This relationship is the **interest rate spread**, and it should narrow as your deposits increase and your credit score rises. If your bank is a credit card issuer, it charges merchants who accept it a few percent on every transaction, and assesses you a hefty interest rate if you don't remit your balance by the due date—thereby earning money at both ends of a transaction. Big revenue also comes from account-maintenance fees, penalties, and ATM charges. Again, these costs should shrink if you're counted among its best customers.

Banks can make a buck by renting safe-deposit boxes and gaining management fees from their trust department as well. What's more, if they're authorized to sell securities and insurance products to financial-planning customers, they'll earn a share of fees and commissions for what their representatives recommend. Lastly, profit is derived from real estate and miscellaneous investments. That pretty much sums up their day.

The joke used to be that if you worked fewer than eight hours, you enjoyed "banker's hours," kidding about the fact that lobbies used to be only open from nine o'clock in the morning to three in the afternoon, and never on weekends. Truth be told, every bank employee, right down to the janitor, was frantically trying to process the day's business when the doors were locked. Automation solved that, but one fact remains the same: When the manager drops the guillotine, the day's business is cut off. That's often (but not exclusively) at two o'clock. All later transactions post to the next day's business, including those occurring on federal holidays and weekends. Therefore, if you were planning to make a deposit after two o'clock to cover the check you wrote to Elizabeth this morning, the teller won't give her lunch money if she shows up at 11:30.

Dollars placed in both savings and checking accounts are classified as **demand deposits**, thereby making these funds available without penalty. Federal law requires banks to stock a fixed percentage of these **liquid funds** to inspire public confidence and to ensure industry stability. Otherwise, a swarm of people making a run on the bank could lead to a crisis, and possible bank failure. (That scenario was part of the story in the classic Christmas movie *It's a Wonderful Life*, with Jimmy Stewart.)

Demand and time deposits are insured against loss by the **Federal Deposit Insurance Corporation** (**FDIC**), which was created following the debacle of the 1929 stock market crash. Currently, the maximum coverage of your combined accounts is $250,000, per insured bank. This implies that when you reach a million dollars, you'd better use four different banks to secure the lot.

Bank names help identify the roles they play in our economy and differentiate them by which governing body is supposed to be keeping an eye on their activity. Your choice is limited to family or corporately owned institutions. Neither the federal government nor any of the fifty states owns a commercial bank. All the following bank types are FDIC-insured.

State Banks

State banks serve towns and neighborhoods, and are chartered and regulated by the states in which they do business—making them smaller by nature than national banks. You'll recognize what you're looking for by names like the First State Bank of Grand Forks and Farmers State Bank. In addition to offering checking, savings, and mortgages, state banks love to offer home-improvement loans. Their favorites are administered by the **Federal Housing Administration (FHA)** and the **US Department of Housing and Urban Development (HUD).** Apply for one of these **Title I programs** if you want to transform a starter house into a comfy home, rental, or resale investment. Qualifying is easy, and terms are favorable. You can do most of the work yourself with some basic carpentry, plumbing, and electrical skills. However, not all people are handy. One exasperated do-it-yourselfer shook his head, saying, "I cut this board off three times, and it's still too short!" Consider hiring contractors to make some or all of the improvements. They should know the building codes.

National Banks

Banks with the word "**national**" in their title, and those with the initials NA (national association) after their names, are institutions guided and regulated by an agency of the US Treasury Department. Examples range from the small Atlanta National Bank to the giant US Bank. The big hitters operate branches from coast to coast, which lets you keep the same-numbered accounts when you move around—even to the far reaches of the globe.

Our country did once have a national bank. Shortly after the American Revolution, the Founding Fathers formed the Bank of North America as part of a comprehensive strategy to transform the new republic into a creditworthy institution. We needed to sell bonds here and abroad to build government structures in the nation's capital and to acquire what was needed to create the equivalent of a business. After this **capitalization** process was finished, the Bank of North America became history. The **Federal Reserve Bank** and the **US Department of the Treasury** are now charged with keeping our nation's currency and finances stable.

Thrifts and Savings-and-Loan Banks

Local **thrift banks** and **savings-and-loan banks** serve as places to save for and finance a house. Mortgages are their business specialty. You can identify one through names like Home Federal Savings and Loan, and Fidelity Federal Savings and Loan. Sadly, thrifts and S&Ls aren't the big players they once were. During the 1980s—a period of high **inflation**, skyrocketing interest rates, an oil embargo, and unfavorable market forces—some executives who ran thrifts and S&Ls used corporate greed and utter mismanagement to cripple the industry. A high percentage of thrifts and savings and loan banks failed, thereby bankrupting the Federal Savings and Loan Insurance Corporation (FSLIC)—the federal agency that had been insuring customer deposits. Congress had to restructure the industry late in the decade, and ultimately, US taxpayers had to bail out the industry. Some executives who were at fault were convicted and went to prison. A combination of federal oversight boards is charged to watch over these operations, and now the FDIC insures them.

Credit Unions

President Franklin Roosevelt made **credit unions** possible by signing the Federal Credit Union Act in 1934, as part of the New Deal legislation. Credit unions differ from banks and S&Ls in the way they're owned and operated, and by which segment of the population they exist to serve. Names like the Navy Federal Credit Union, Duluth Teachers Credit Union, and the Polish & Slavic Federal Credit Union erase all doubt as to who that might be. To join a credit union, you must meet its specific eligibility requirement, which is spelled out in its **FOM** or **field of membership**.

As you can infer from the above names, not everyone qualifies. Many Christian denominations have formed these **financial cooperatives** to serve their faithful, including Thrivent Federal Credit Union for Lutherans, Catholic United Financial, and America's Christian Credit Union.

The National Credit Union Administration (NCUA) regulates federal credit unions and insures member funds, which are known as **credit union shares**. Individual states charter local credit unions, but don't insure their holdings. Instead, these credit unions choose the NCUA or American Share Insurance (ASI), a private insurer, as their protector of deposits.

Credit union members themselves own these nonprofit organizations and are steered by a board of directors, comprised of the same. Instead of sole profitability, their stated objective is to provide members with lower-cost car and consumer loans, and home financing. Often, their savings accounts (which they call **share accounts**) yield a higher return than do banks, and their checking accounts (or **share draft accounts**) may have may lower account maintenance fees. Competitive credit unions have a fairly wide surcharge-free ATM network, as many banks do.

This summarizes your banking options—and options they are. You don't need their services to get by. There's always the cash basis.

Working on a Cash Basis

Working on a **cash basis** is the oldest method of running the business of your life, though not always the most convenient. We all start generating income by mowing lawns, waiting tables, and holding various part-time jobs. Our first expenses typically revolve around meals, fashion, entertainment, phone, and Internet-access costs. If that's you, my guess is that things have been working fairly well so far—cash is king.

A great number of people swore by that truth following the Great Depression, which left many banks **insolvent**, thereby nuking depositor accounts. Tragically, some victims leaped from heights. Trust evaporated, and countless individuals and families reverted to the all-cash lifestyle—renouncing banks forever. Many actually buried their savings in backyard coffee cans. There is little doubt that, even today—in some old houses, beneath trapdoors or in cluttered attic corners—there are still caches of money that have been orphaned by owners who have died or lost their marbles.

I'm a strong proponent of encouraging sane juniors and seniors like you to stay a while longer with the tactical advantages of cash. There should be no rush to jump into full-service banking until budgeting has been mastered. If you don't know how to make ends meet by working with dollar bills, then paying maintenance fees and suffering bank overdraft charges will only make your shortage worse.

Let's examine the banking-alternative financial instruments, which are purposely designed to facilitate the mechanics of the cash basis, whether you're purchasing and paying bills in person, online, or by mail.

The Money Order

A **money order**, whether postal or commercial, resembles, and acts like, a check. It's safe, economical, and preferable to merchants than a personal check. The example shown in Figure 4-1 is available at any postal branch. Simply fill in your payee's name after the clerk embosses your specific dollar amount. Its serial-numbered receipt serves as a record and is, as the document states, "your guarantee for a refund if your money order is lost or stolen, provided you fill in the Pay To and From information. . . ." Should you need proof of payment, the postmaster can trace it.

Money orders also work well for maintaining privacy. For example, if you're so inclined to donate to a cause but don't want to have your name and address shared with a bunch of other charities, send a money order without your personal information. That will keep you off mailing lists.

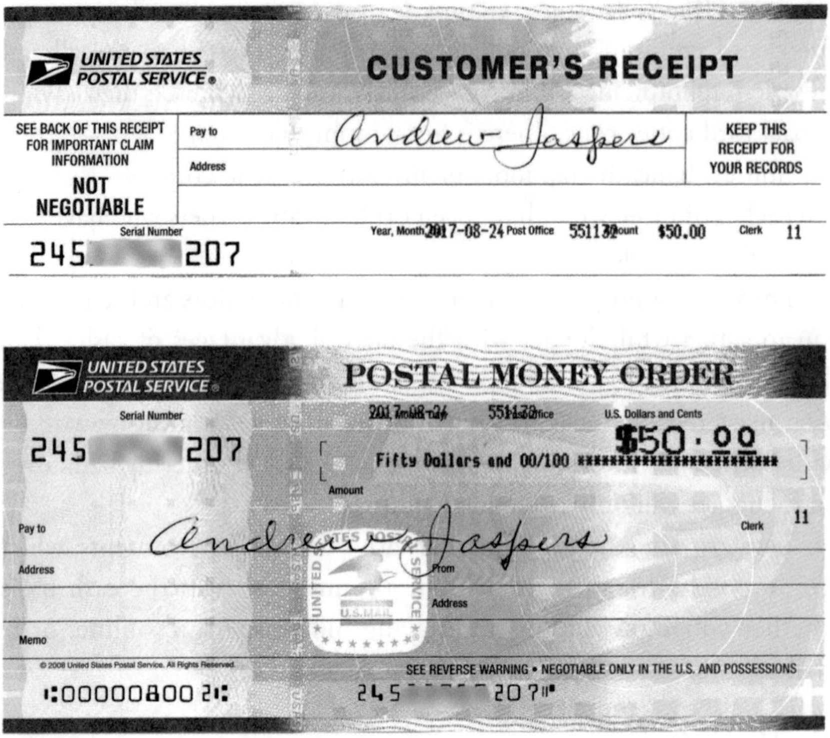

Figure 4-1   Money Order

The Wire Transfer

Western Union became a household name by sending messages via tele-graph wire. In time, network offices were structured to allow money transfers by wire within the day. Even today, financial houses, banks, and individuals utilize wire transfers to move money around quickly. Many a young Hollywood actor has dodged a bullet before high noon with an emergency money wire from Dad in Boston—no Internet con-nection required. If you aren't near a Western Union office, you can send or receive a wire transfer at many banks, drugstores, and superstores.

But the above aren't useful on the Web. Bonnie and Clyde certainly couldn't have imagined such a thing. Unlike them, you're witnessing the gradual replacement of brick-and-mortar stores, as the world buys out of thin air. The modern cyberworld has its own villains and challenges—hacking, scams, identity theft, ransomware, and the vulnerability of the satellites which makes this universe possible. To spend their larcenous gains, crooks are increasingly turning to the cryptocurrency **bitcoin**, and trying to exploit any of its weaknesses in an attempt to cover their tracks. Heavy regulation is sure to come, even if bitcoin stays around.

Gift Cards and Prepaid Debit Cards

Until you reach the age of majority and can qualify for a credit card, you have two options to buy online. One is to ask a parent or guardian to make the Web purchase and simultaneously fork over the money. If you view that as a demonstration of competent budgeting, it might soothe the ego of someone whose independence is still emerging.

Your other option is to purchase a gift card or a prepaid debit card. A **gift card** is a cash replacement, which can be redeemed for goods and services at an endless variety of restaurants and retailers. Some can be used wherever major credit cards are accepted. The $25 American Express gift card shown in Figure 4-2 is an example. Higher denominations are available, and cards are ready to go after the retailer activates them. The card shown here costs about $4, but it is a one-time fee. Funds on the card don't expire, yet the card is valid for only five years; if money remains past the date shown, you can get a fresh card with the amount posted to it. Meanwhile, if the gift card is lost or stolen, remaining funds can be replaced through customer service. You can also check the balance online. This card is not redeemable for cash and can't be used at an ATM. Gift cards like this one also come with a cardholder agreement—which should be read, as with every type of card below.

A **debit card** reduces your account balance as you use it. For instance, if your boss gives you a card to fill the tank on a company vehicle, it's a debit card. Banks, too, offer debit cards to access checking or savings, and nonbanking spots provide one as an integral part of a stand-alone financial tool. The VISA green dot card shown in Figure 4-3 is one example of this.

Figure 4-2   American Express Gift Card

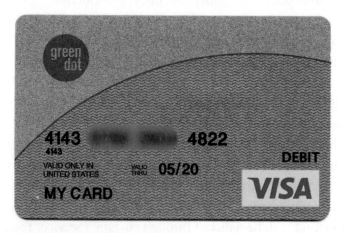

Figure 4-3   Green Dot Card

Upon purchase, the retailer posts your cash to the card—making it a **prepaid** (debit) **card**. The VISA green dot (good for about three years) has a number of features and benefits. For instance, the instrument is reloadable when empty (for a fee) and offers the option of accepting your entire payroll check. You can also access cash at an ATM, often for a fee plus whatever the bank or ATM owner charges you. Additionally, the issuer may deduct a monthly fee, whether the card is used or not.

As you can see, all these costs can get expensive. Prepaids are suitable in the short run for any young person but are quickly dropped by people who get their financial act together and are qualified for a credit card. People who don't advance are unmercifully punished forever with fees and penalties. The poor—in that sense—must pay more to live.

The Credit Card and Charge Card

There is no such thing as a "green dot credit card." A **credit card** represents an unsecured **revolving line of credit** that has an upper limit. By definition, you aren't required to make a fixed payment amount each month but can vary your remittance. Credit cards do require a pretty small minimum payment each month and come with a wide range of interest rates. Debts with fixed payments, such as a car loan, are known as **installment loans**. The comedian Stephen Wright once said, "If you think nobody cares about you, try missing a couple of payments." Finally, a **charge card** is an in-store credit-purchasing arrangement that you can't use elsewhere.

You can't purchase a credit card; all you can do is apply for one. The better your credit rating, the more likely you'll be approved. Establishing your good name begins with demonstrating the ability to pay your bills on time and accumulating financial reserves. With a good track record of payments, you'll receive higher-limit and lower-interest-rate offers. Information about you is detailed on your credit report, and credit offers are driven by your **FICO** score, which will be covered in detail in the bankruptcy chapter.

However, there is such a thing as a **secured credit card**. It can be of assistance in establishing credit and when rehabilitating after bankruptcy. Some companies, such as Capital One, will issue a secured MasterCard after you place funds in their interest-bearing savings account. Card purchases can't exceed this collateral, but the more you save with the issuer, the higher you set your spending limit.

You'll need a credit card sooner or later. You can't make air, hotel, or car-rental reservations by phone or Web without one. But the financial world can't oblige you yet; the law states that it's a criminal offense for banks to extend a line of credit to minors. This proclamation protects both parties. In addition, Internet bank sites must be careful not to violate any part of the **Children's Online Privacy Protection Act** (COPPA), which is aimed at protecting those under thirteen.

In an effort to get a personalized card into your hands, some banks have developed a legal agreement financially tied to your parent or guardian's account. Banks theorize that card usage teaches nearly minted adults how to use credit responsibly. Really? Doesn't this supposition put the cart in front of a filly or colt that isn't yet trained to pull it? In the first place, you shouldn't be put in the position of having to juggle debt. That shouldn't occur until you're well past financial stability, which is prefaced by an outstanding ability to budget.

We don't take incurring debt lightly. Any time you borrow, you surrender a portion of your power and control to the lender—moving you back one more row on the bus.

Moreover, should it really be the banking industry's role to educate you? It sounds much like the fox guarding the henhouse.

The Cashier's Check

A **cashier's check** is our last cash-handling tool. It's professional-grade, and certified to be as "good as gold." Procuring one solves the problem of carrying, or mailing, a large sum of cash. When you ask, a bank teller deposits your funds into a special account and uses a check printer to create this multicopy instrument. An instance when you might want one is that of buying a higher-dollar item, like a car, from a private party. A smart seller should decline a personal check, but have no trouble accepting this bank issuance. The best bank customers receive a cashier's check for free, but the rest usually must pay a per-hundred-dollar charge.

However, cashier's checks are restricted to bank customers. So, here's the good news: You are hereby invited to become one as soon as the doors are open tomorrow. Your first order of business will be establishing a cash reserve. Before we continue with that, it's wise to discuss title law, because it pertains to one of the first questions asked on an account application.

Title Law

Your degree of ownership in an asset is conveyed to the world by a concept called **title**. This invisible claim to exclusive possession serves the same purpose as an automobile title, which is a fancy sheet of paper. Practically nothing else you own has a hard-copy title. Instead, we simply claim ownership by mere possession, with society operating under the assumption that we've come by it honestly. As the saying goes, "Possession is nine-tenths of the law."

Funds deposited into a bank account require a descriptive form of title because you have now trustingly put them into the bank's possession. That corporate body is now on the hook for safely keeping your dollars in a numbered account and restricting access. The collegiate term that defines this relationship is **fiduciary**.

Individual title is established by simply checking that box. Everyone else on earth is now excluded from gaining access without a court order. You can, though, list someone else as an **authorized signer**. Then, if you break your arm, Mom can sign your checks, but this side note doesn't alter your ownership status.

Here's another example: If it was Grandma's individual account, and she dies **intestate** (without a will), her account goes to **probate court**, along with everything else she owns. There, a judge will determine who will inherit her money, sewing machine, and Buick, based on the number and kinship of her family members, and claims by best friends, the maid, the butler, etc. That litigation process could take a long time—especially if people are scattered all over creation.

Listing a beneficiary on your account application keeps assets out of probate court. Sometimes a **beneficiary designation** is referred to as **POD**, or **payable on death; TOD**, or **transfer on death**, is commonly used for securities such as stocks and bonds. Your first exercise in **estate**

planning, then, is to list a beneficiary who would theoretically inherit your account(s).

Joint tenancy is designed to protect the ownership rights and give unobstructed access to two or more individuals. Minors and parents frequently choose this form of title for a number of reasons. It's also perfect for married couples, but it may be downright foolhardy for unrelated people to hold title jointly. For example, suppose Jerry, Max, Phil, and Don rent a house while at college, and they each pitch money into jointly held checking for his share of rent, utilities, etc. Everything is fine until Max writes a check to make up his past-due car payments rather than paying the rent. Worse yet, Don could skip town with the entire balance. It may be difficult to have either arrested for stealing, or to prove that fact in court. After all, the jointly held title gives all signers a legal right to access the dough. Your best defense, when renting with others, is to make your share of rent payable to the property owner, using either your checking account or a money order—but never, ever cash.

Another bombshell that can wreck your joint account is a court judgment against your joint-account holder. Let's say Bert and Ernie pool their savings and equally have $5,000 in an account. One day, Bert messes up and receives a $10,000 judgment against him. Law allows for seizure of the entire account if none of Bert's other assets will satisfy the claim. This is known as an **invasion of assets**. Ernie will lose his entire investment, even though the poor guy is innocent.

Lastly, many people are kicking themselves this very day for putting their live-in boyfriend or girlfriend on a mortgage. Though it's not for me to address such a relationship here, it is critical to know that in a breakup, they remain joined at the hip. They're tied together by debt repayment terms, have an intermingling of credit histories, and have to deal with who gets the interest deduction on their tax return. Yuck.

When you check the **JTWROS** application box, all parties listed are considered to have **joint tenancy with rights of survivorship**.

Therefore, if you only listed your friend Billy, your account assets would go directly to him if you died prematurely, thus cutting out Mom, Dad, and your little sister. Again, Billy can go to the bank and empty your account anytime he wishes. Some jurisdictions follow **common law**, and the implications of joint tenancy will vary. Moreover, adults should not title assets with their parents. Keep finances separate to avoid being drawn into someone else's judgments, liens, and foreclosures.

Custodial title is designed to benefit you, as a minor. The **Uniform Gifts to Minors Act** (**UGMA**) allows benefactors—such as your parents, guardians, or rich aunt—to deposit their gifts of cash, annuities, stocks, and bonds into an account with your name on it. The benefactor has sole management and control over the account, and proceeds won't be yours until you reach legal age. The downside is that you're now liable for tax on earnings. Fortunately, you're eligible for an offsetting credit, which you'll read about in Chapter 6. The **Uniform Transfers to Minors Act** (**UTMA**) allows your godfather, Uncle Dimitri, to generously transfer his book royalties, valuable artwork, or real estate to you, and receive a tax break for both of you. (Nice guy, that Uncle Dimitri.) Again, age restrictions apply. UGMA and UTMA rules differ a bit across the nation, so it's imperative that benefactors consult with tax advisors. Equally important, assets titled this way affect the level of student-loan financing.

Custodial accounts work well for college savings. Of course, this doesn't mean that every teen pays for college tuition with the funds—some brats buy sports cars instead. If that was a concern ahead of time, the donor could have set up a special trust account with specific stipulations.

Consult an attorney or CPA for advice on how to title an asset.

The Cash Reserve

With title behind us, we return to establishing your cash reserve, which is a necessary, powerful personal asset. The rally cry of Minnesota's TCF

Bank was once "Tuck a Buck a Day Away." Inflation may have made the slogan obsolete, but the basic message endures.

Savings accounts offer a path of least resistance. Critics argue, though, that these demand accounts don't generate much interest, making them poor investments. The faultfinders are correct, but miss the point entirely. A cash reserve is not intended to be an investment in any way, shape, or form. It's your buffer, your shock absorber; it's your financial firewall. The words self-define its intrinsic value, not its earning power. If gaining a good return is the prime motivator for buying non-cash personal assets, then critics have to include your leather sectional and big-screen TV, neither of which earns interest, and both of which decline sharply in value on day two. Pawnshop owners love cash-reserve-free people—especially those who buy the very best product brands. Customers walk out with a fraction of what they had invested and end up with nothing to sit on to watch what's no longer there.

Financial planners tout the cash reserve as part of risk management, but they can't claim to be the authors of the philosophy. Go to Genesis 41 to understand the concept by extension. In attribution to God, Joseph interpreted Pharaoh's dreams—and, with unwavering confidence in what he had heard, Egypt's ruler ordered national leaders to follow Joseph's instructions in preparation for the coming seven years of famine. They did, as you recall, and Egypt consolidated its position as a regional power. Cash is king.

Purchase your cash reserve on the installment plan by setting something aside each month. You'll know how much is available when you work out your budget. Or, if you feel like saving seems like a chore, then simply spend less. This route takes less effort and you can describe yourself as "prudently inactive."

Establishing one of the following as a cash reserve gives you the freedom to cash payroll checks without paying a fee. In addition, as a customer you're granted free access to your bank's coin-counting machines. You might even find a good cup of coffee in the lobby.

Types of Savings Accounts

The Passbook Account

The venerable, but beleaguered, passbook savings account is still available. At one time, passbook savings was the A-1 vehicle citizens utilized to collectively amass a vast sum in thrifts and S&Ls across the country. Borrowing from this great cauldron, families were able to finance modest yet comfortable homes. This pattern fueled the home-building industry, which grew along with the return of GIs and the prosperity that developed after World War II.

With the development of the savings products outlined below, passbook savings accounts are nearly obsolete, yet they remain an excellent tool for a tween to learn the basics of saving.

The Conventional Account

Conventional savings is now the standard type of savings account. It offers a stated rate of interest, which can increase or decrease gradually as the Federal Reserve tightens or loosens interest rates. The investment comes with a pad of deposit/withdrawal slips and a **transaction register**. Your bank mails (or emails) a monthly statement, which can usually also be accessed online. Compare the transactions that the bank shows with your register records. Then, add your newly earned interest and record any monthly maintenance charge in your register. The opening minimum is usually the rough equivalent of a few days' pay. You can access your money in person, at an ATM, and/or by using a debit card. If, and when, you bank online, you can view your balance and activity and make transfers.

The Money Market Account

A **money market account** is a second-tier cash reserve, which pays a floating, higher rate of interest. It may also come with a register and a pad of numbered **drafts**, which look and act like checks. However, a money market isn't designed to be used for regular checking. Banks restrict you to writing a few drafts per month, otherwise you'll incur a penalty fee. This account fits nicely with a home-improvement loan. The proceeds go in as a lump sum, and then you draft out to pay for building materials, or to settle with a contractor for a completed remodeling stage.

The Certificate of Deposit

A **CD** is a **certificate of deposit**. Because this investment is classified as a **time deposit**, it's intended to remain undisturbed until maturity. In packaging CDs, banks purchase higher-yielding investments—such as government long bonds and corporate debt offerings—and essentially break down the total into smaller, roundly numbered, affordable bundles. This strategy allows banks to pass on part of the higher yield to you, and still make a profit. Banks formerly required a $100,000 investment (a **jumbo certificate**), but now minimums are as low as $5,000 or less. Terms vary from any number of years to as few as ninety days. Longer terms and larger deposits lead to higher returns. Typically, you won't receive any interest until the CD matures. If you opt to withdraw your money before the party's over, you'll forfeit at least a sizable portion of your profit.

Paying Bills with Smartphone Apps

The digital financial services industry has taken on traditional consumer banking. At your fingertips are payment services, such as PayPal, which are tied to a credit card, that you ultimately pay off by check. This makes that and other financial apps the third layer upon cold, hard cash. Major technology companies such as Amazon, Apple, and Google have gotten into the act, because it's convenient for you and profitable for them. Each app purchase generates a bit of money for someone along the line, which inevitably results in higher product and service costs. As this new layer of consumerism develops, FinTechs will experience their share of scandals and consumer losses. Predictably, heavier government **regulation** probably isn't far behind.

Checking Account Basics

One day, it's probable that the Internet will be available in the farthest corners of the earth, and that the vast majority of the world will do its banking online, using handheld devices—or even by surgical implant into the forearm. Even today, people look at the balance on their digital screens and believe that the shown amount is what they have available to spend. Some are correct, primarily because they know what they're doing. Others assume that the bank knows what the depositor is doing and give you a blank stare when asked how to explain that—or what's going to happen to the balance tomorrow.

The challenge is to stay in the black while simultaneously writing checks, using debit cards, paying bills online, using apps, and utilizing automatic payments (which effectively reduce your ability to time payments). This multitude of methods makes keeping track of an account balance tricky at best. The bank will keep you informed about how well you do—often in the form of an overdraft charge if you don't do it well. You'll fall into the first group by getting the basics of checking down pat. Here we go.

Opening a Checking Account

By signing a checking account agreement, you authorize the bank to pay your creditors in the order they receive checks or bill-pay requests. To document the events, each bank is obligated to furnish you with a monthly statement, which gives you a chronological record of the details. Increasingly, banks want to send this record by email; if you don't provide a digital address, some banks have the gall to charge you for a paper statement.

Though reluctant to say so, the bank doesn't want you writing many checks because higher volume requires more employees. (Various self-checkout aisles reduce the number of human cashiers, as well.) In fact, if some bankers could have it their way, all checks would be eliminated. To that end, the industry adopted the debit card and automatic-payment technology.

Typically, twenty-five dollars will open an account. Your initial package includes **temporary checks**; a transaction register; and a flimsy plastic cover that holds them both. An optional genuine-leather cover lends dignity to your earnings and lasts for years, but costs about thirty bucks. (Put this upgrade on your Christmas wish list.) Your temporary checks are numbered in very low digits, but your first order usually begins with check 101. It is permissible, however, to ask that it start at 301, or higher; this way, you'll appear to be more experienced.

If you run out of temporary checks before your custom checks arrive, the bank will provide you with generic **counter checks**. In fact, this substitute is always available, as long as you have ID and your account number. Check-printing companies offer a variety of check styles and colors, with some being more expensive than others. Customer-friendly banks additionally offer **counterfeit-evident checks**, along with **security pens** and access to a security website. (If you didn't know, crooks can wash regular ballpoint ink off a written check and fill in a new amount payable to themselves. Do an Internet search on "check washing.")

The cost of your initial order will be debited immediately to (subtracted from) your account, so record it in your register to reflect this decline. The same holds true with the first month's maintenance fee. Those facts sailed over my head when I opened my first account, and I bounced a check before the ink was dry!

Check out the sample check in Figure 4-4. Protect your account identity by limiting the amount of personal data printed in the upper-left-hand corner. Technically, nothing needs to go there, but going to that extreme will cause you problems elsewhere. The bank identifies you by your account number, which appears in the **code line** at the bottom of your check. The first nine digits within this string of numbers is your ABA (American Bankers Association) **bank routing number**. After the code break is your account number. Following the final code break is your check number as it appears in Arabic numerals in the document's upper-right-hand corner.

Figure 4-4 Sample Check. (Courtesy of Deluxe Check.)

At some point in the future, you'll forget to record a check in your register, which makes striking an accurate balance impossible. You can avoid the frustration in two ways. First of all, don't write a check before putting it in the register. Nevertheless, we all forget—especially when in a hurry. Secondly, a failsafe is ordering checks that create a carbonless copy on NCR paper.

To use the register as designed, record all transactions on separate lines and jot their amounts under the appropriate column headings, as in Figure 4-5. Each column is labeled in the language that banks

How to use your transaction register

NUMBER OR CODE	DATE	TRANSACTION DESCRIPTION	PAYMENT, FEE WITHDRAWAL (-)		✓ FEE	DEPOSIT, CREDIT (+)		$ BALANCE	
			$			$		$	
124	7/1	Dry Cleaners	16	15				310	97
ATM	7/3	Cash withdrawal	40	00				270	97
AP	7/5	Gas & Electric	65	23				205	74
DC	7/6	ABC Grocery	59	43				146	31
125	7/8	Dentist	10	00				136	31
AD	7/9	Automatic Deposit				300	00	436	31

Column headings: DC Debit Card | ATM Teller Withdrawal | AD Automatic Deposit | AP Automatic Payment | BP Online Bill Pay | T Online or Phone Transfer

Fill in the check number or transaction code, date and a description of the transaction. Record the amount of the transaction in the appropriate column. The ✓ column is used for checking off transactions that are listed on your monthly statement.

- **DC** Debit Card
- **ATM** Teller Withdrawal
- **AD** Automatic Deposit
- **AP** Automatic Payment
- **BP** Online Bill Pay
- **T** Online or Phone Transfer

Figure 4-5 Register Interior. (Courtesy of Deluxe Check.)

and accountants speak. **Generally Accepted Accounting Principles (GAAP)** dictate that items leaving checking are called **debits** (-). **Debit transactions** include honored checks, ATM withdrawals, automatic payments, fund transfers out, service charges, and fees. Dollars going in are termed **credits** (+). **Credit transactions** are typically your deposits, fund transfers in, and account interest. The register's narrow column with a checkmark symbol is used during your bank reconciliation (i.e., when you confirm each deposit/payment amount).

Document your register by filling in all the outside blanks, and serialize it with #1 at the same time, as in Figure 4-6. Doing so will help you find old information someday. Place all filled registers in with your corresponding bank statements and mark the fresh one as #2. And leave three or four register lines blank between each month's activities; this allows for inevitable additions or corrections.

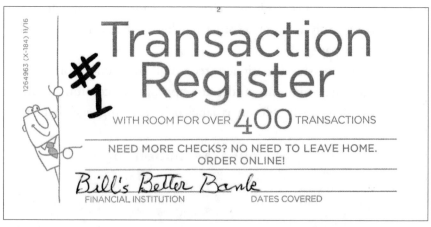

Figure 4-6   Register Exterior

Here's another tip: Leave an auditing footprint for yourself by writing your check number and dollar amount on the corresponding invoice or statement (as in Figure 4-7), and slip it in your "Paid Bills" file jacket, where ATM withdrawal slips and debit-card receipts go.

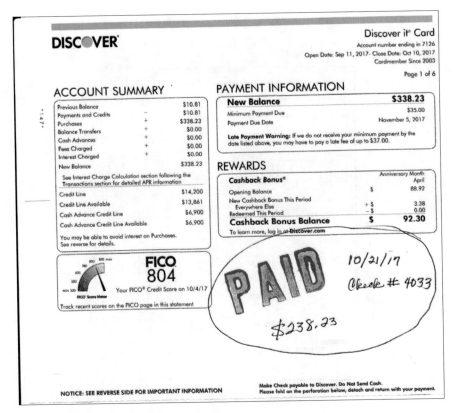

Figure 4-7   Paid Statement

Incidentally, an original bill from a seller is called an **invoice**. Characteristically, invoices are serial-numbered, as in figure 4-8. Doing so uniquely distinguishes identical purchases made at different times. By contrast, a **monthly statement** is a recap of all invoices, payments, and/ or adjustments. For example, the Discover card statement shown gives a total all of the charges during the month but doesn't provide any details about what was bought. In the case of, say, your Internet service, the original invoice was the account agreement you signed, whereas your monthly statement serves as a recap of transactions and the manner in which you paid.

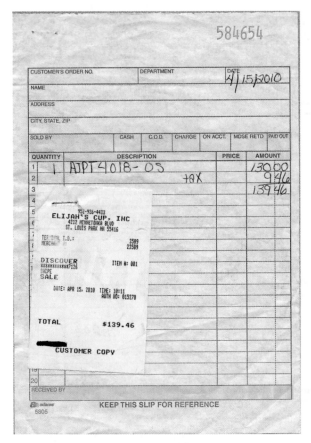

Figure 4-8   Sample Invoice

Endorsing a Check

A written check is negotiable instrument, implying that it can be passed from individual to individual until it's ultimately cashed or deposited. Its final disposition is determined by the last **check endorsement,** or signature on the back. When you sign your name on the back as payee, this gives the payor (your employer, for example) proof that you received it and at which bank it was processed. Signing your name *only* is a **blank endorsement**, and leaves the check "live" (see Figure 4-9). If you give it afterward to someone else as a payment, that person can sign their name below yours—making it a **second-party check.**

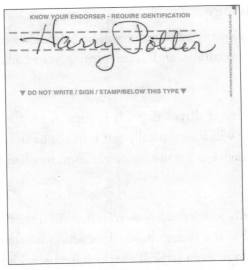

Figure 4-9   Check with Blank Endorsement

For any check you intend to deposit in the future, write "For deposit only," as a first step, below your signature. This **conditional endorsement** shown in Figure 4-10 helps safeguard your check until you get it to the bank. When you get to the bank and fill out your deposit slip, add your account number as the second step. You can still get a portion of it in cash, if you indicate that on your deposit slip.

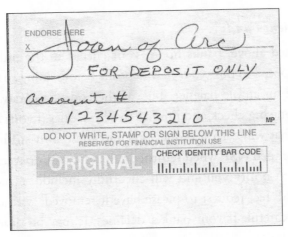

Figure 4-10   Check with Conditional Endorsement

Bank Terminology

Knowing the following bank terms will be helpful in recording transactions, avoiding overdrafts, and in performing your bank reconciliation:

Direct Deposit

Your employer has a **direct deposit** request form for payroll checks. Completing one will automatically put it in the bank on or before payday. All you'll receive is a non-negotiable copy attached to your stub.

Deposit Holds

Banks temporarily restrict access to your deposit if they aren't positive it will be honored at the issuer's bank. This action is known as a **deposit hold**. Of all things, even payroll checks have been known to bounce. If you're at a window, the teller (or ATM) typically tells you when your funds will be available. That date may also be printed on your receipt, and sometimes the bank will double up by notifying you by mail. Any check written against a held deposit is returned to your payee and will bear **Uncollected Funds** stamped in red ink across its face. Quite likely, your payee will incur a bank charge, as well as you. The only way to avoid the whole situation is keeping a balance higher than the held deposit.

Non-Sufficient Funds

As mentioned above, banks honor your checks in the order received, and are supposed to post your new deposits before doing so. Everything is cool with an ample balance, but, at the end of the day, a sly bank might pay one big check and bounce five little ones if your account is a bit short. That will earn it money. Each of these **non-sufficient funds** checks is stamped **NSF** when returned unpaid to your payee. Your bank is required to notify you and will cheerfully include a charge. If you suffer an NSF fee, request to please have it removed, with the promise to be more careful. If your banker declines, it may be time to change dance partners.

Banks offer "overdraft protection." You can preauthorize them to transfer money from savings into checking to cover deficits as they occur. If you qualify for their credit card, overdraft amounts can also be added to that.

Bank Authorizations and Automatic Payments

A **bank authorization** (**BA**) or **automatic payment** (**AP**) is your written instruction to move an agreed sum from one of your accounts to a vendor on a specific day of the month, which will continue until you ask that it be stopped. I have this setup with my life insurance. It isn't likely that I'll be on safari in Africa for six months, but, no matter where I am, I know that my policy won't lapse if my memory does (despite any reminder notices in the mail). Companies you do business with have the forms.

Electronic Funds Transfer (EFT)

An **Electronic Funds Transfer** (**EFT**) does exactly what it sounds that it should. For instance, if you call the bank and ask to have money moved from one account to another, a rep will hit a button, and the deed is done. When you bank online, you can usually do this yourself.

Automated Clearing House (ACH)

The **Automated Clearing House** (**ACH**) is a countrywide network of computers that financial institutions use to process payments electronically. It is fast and efficient, and makes direct deposit possible.

Here's an illustration of how the ACH can impact your account: Let's say that you mailed a check to a payment center, and figured that it'll take four days or so before it would get back to your bank for collection. Maybe so, maybe not. If the payment center is set up on the ACH network, it will simply slip your check into a reader that converts the information into an electronic-payment request, which it will send to your bank with lightning speed. Afterward, your paper check is shredded.

Floating and Kiting a Check

While the mail carrier has your check on the way to the payment center, it is "floating." **Check float** is a cog in the monetary system's wheel, and using it is all right. However, trying to take undue advantage of this downtime may backfire. If your strategy in the above scenario was getting your payment in by the due date to avoid a penalty, but you didn't have enough in checking, you might have figured you had a few extra days to make a covering deposit because of the time normally required to make a round trip. You're likely to receive an NSF if the payment center is on the ACH, because this will cut two or more days off your "end-around."

Check kiting is outright bank fraud. Here's an example: Suppose Sam doesn't have enough money to cover a check, so he says to Robert, "Dude, deposit $100 from your checking into my account, so that I'm covered." Robert comes back with, "Hey buddy, I don't have enough in mine to do that. But tell you what: I'll write that check into your account if you write one back to mine for the same amount. We could keep passing the buck back and forth for days!" You think so? Good luck, boys. Hope you don't look fat in horizontal stripes.

In essence, these characters have taken out short, interest-free bank loans. Although we're not talking about much money, this disrupts the free flow in the monetary system. If millions of people tried this every day, it could put our banks at risk and increase their operating costs. After all, banks must often borrow money overnight from reserve banks to meet their federally mandated liquidity percentages. The industry refers to these loans as **short-term paper**, or "paper" for short. Banks pay interest on this paper.

Postdated Checks

Let me tell you about Carl, whose rent was late—again. Jill, the property owner, wanted an immediate resolution. He knew that he'd have it by the next week, so he handed her a **postdated** check, and asked her to hold it until then. Jill agreed, but changed her mind and immediately dropped it in her bank. The result? Carl got a $35 NSF fee, and Jill wound up with a worthless check that she could take to small-claims court (conciliation court). Her real intention was to start eviction proceedings, as she was over his antics.

In most American jurisdictions, Carl's check would technically become legal tender when he handed it off, regardless of the check date. Existing state laws regarding postdated checks can be vague, and interpretations can vary. (The same holds true for stale date checks, which we'll get to shortly.)

I'll have you know that Jill has two other cards to play before she takes Carl to court. Our wise property owner (or you, by extension) can call or visit the culprit's bank and inquire if the NSF is now good because of a recent deposit, such as a tax refund or payroll check. If the teller confirms this, Jill can present the worthless check and collect right there. If the teller responds in the negative, Jill can repeat the inquiry as often as she'd like, as long as Carl's account remains open. But constant negative replies become an exercise in frustration. Her other ace in the hole is writing a letter of instruction to Carl's bank, asking it to send her a certified check as soon as funds become available in his account—which could be months away. This process is called **entering a check for collection**, which is a little-known, but valuable, option.

Rules and procedures differ by bank and state Uniform Commercial Codes.

Stale Date Checks

Many refer to an uncashed check written about six months earlier as a **stale date check**, and consider it worthless. Wrong. Gone are the days when a clerk analyzed each check for valid dates and authorized signatures. Banks now have code-line readers and scanners to accomplish the job. Technology has seen to it that a stale date check can sail right through, despite computer programs that look for out-of-sequence check numbers. Again, state laws vary in their treatment of stale date checks.

Stop Payment Request

There is a situation when you may not want the bank to honor a specific check. If you feel that someone is cheating you, you can submit a **stop payment request** for that particular check. For a fee, the bank will do everything it can to intercept it—which is why it's called a "request." In some states, your order must be in writing—so, you'd better get moving. A stop payment is generally good for no more than six months. If you want to renew it, you'll start over and pay another fee. If you had paid by credit card, you have the right to call that card's customer-service department and dispute the transaction. It will suspend payment on that obligation, and an investigation will start.

I can't think of another reason to use a stop payment request. We did, years back, if a check was lost—perhaps in the mail. Not these days. Here's a true story: I once wrote a check to a guy for roughly $1,600. A few days later, he said he'd lost it. Before I was so inclined to replace it, I dropped by my bank, thinking that I might fill out a request form. My wise banker, Patti Krieger, said, "No. Your account's security has been compromised. If a crook finds it, he might be able to buy online, using your personal info and our code line. And there are other ways. Let's close your checking and open a new account with a different number." She then hit the computer key that prevented any transaction from occurring in my account. That **account freeze** meant that not even I could use it.

Closing an Account

Patti sat me down with her right-hand gal, Gudrun, and the two of us did the final bank reconciliation. Between her real-time computer records and my up-to-date, balanced register, we could identify four **outstanding checks**. I wanted those to clear, so we left enough in my original account to cover them and moved the balance into a new account with a different number. As each outstanding check showed up, a clerk hand-processed it. In the end, everything came out to the penny, and that ended that.

Just remember that you can't close your account until it's been reconciled. Someone might come out short—and, I assure you, it won't be the bank.

When Terror Strikes

Someday, you won't be able to find your debit card or checkbook. You don't know if it's been misplaced or stolen. If a thorough search leaves you empty-handed, notify your bank right away—the two of you can figure out what to do next.

A smart banker will give you good advice, but here's a true story of one who didn't: A woman had her purse stolen; and her checkbook, ID, and wallet were inside. When she and her husband notified the bank, a rep said, "Don't worry. We'll handle it." Well, the thief was smarter than the banker and was finding ways to weasel them out of thousands of dollars. Meanwhile, the couple's financial affairs were messy. In the end, Funky Federal had to cough up the money to cover the losses because it hadn't performed its **fiduciary responsibility** correctly. The bank should have advised freezing and closing the account.

Fees and Penalties

Before we wrap up, it's only fair to hardworking, honest bankers to have a philosophical chat about charging fees and penalties—especially for an NSF. Years ago, I wondered how and why banks and merchants got away with charging them. I figured that if I made a bookkeeping error and made good on my bad check, there should be no harm and no foul. Maybe in an honest world that's how things should work, but there's always somebody who yields to the devil's temptation. Because of clowns like this, the law has made writing **worthless checks** illegal—whether by accident or on purpose.

Will Officer Martha enforce the law? The answer lies in how she views it. If a burglar steals your TV, you can call her, and she'll try to arrest and jail the criminal. But if you sell that same TV to Joe, who writes you a bad check, she has the tendency to tell you it's a civil matter, and that you should go to court. If you're ever in that situation, try to stand your ground. Authorities avoid rubber checks like the plague. Too many are written every day, and fraud can be difficult to prove beyond the shadow of a doubt. People plead oversight and, in some cases, pure incompetence. Sometimes that's true. To complicate matters, merchants and banks rarely have the time or resources to go to court for twenty bucks. This makes Sally's Salad Bar hesitate to take your check. In fact, I can't think of a restaurant that will. Criminal judges don't like bad checks, either. If each bad check were prosecuted, courtrooms would be the size of football fields. Look to your state's worthless-check law to learn how such matters are handled.

By charging fees and imposing penalties for messing up what should have been a smooth transaction, banks and merchants can help offset unrecoverable losses. Moreover, just the threat acts as a deterrent. But if you think your bank goes overboard, it may be time to change partners again.

Meanwhile, Satan thinks this three-ring circus is just hilarious, and is dreaming up new ways to tempt us into believing that more material things will make us happy. If you want to see what a zealous quest for money produces, look back to the stock market crash of 1929 and the Great Depression that followed. Bank failures occurred, in large part, because these institutions had intermingled personal accounts with securities accounts, which is risky business. When stock values plummeted during the sell-off, the mixed pot went dry before mom and pop could withdraw their money and stock sellers could be paid. A provision of the US Banking Act of 1933 (also called the **Glass-Steagall Act**) forced the separation of investment and private banking. Congress established the FDIC in the same year to henceforth insure customer accounts.

History repeated itself in the 1980s with the S&L crisis, and most recently with the mortgage-lending collapse as this century got under way. Because of greed and deception in some elements of the private sector and misguided economic policies in parts of the public sector, taxpayers in the middle ultimately had to bail out the calamities in both cases. It's no wonder that many pray to St. Michael the Archangel to defend us in battle.

In review, we've considered the advantages of the cash basis and studied bank types, bank products, and the industry's financial services. But you don't have to settle on just one option. It's not uncommon for individuals and couples to have savings here and checking there—perhaps even four or more accounts at various locations—and still be great at managing currency.

As you progress, consider evaluating faith-based organizations and credit unions. And down the road, keep in mind that smart business owners lock up their commercial checkbooks and bank statements when not in use. Furthermore, personal banking information should stay at home. There are too many horror stories about employees who embezzle.

Helpful Links

Federal Deposit Insurance Corporation
https://www.fdic.gov

FHA and HUD
https://www.hud.gov/program_offices/housing/fhahistory

Federal Reserve System
https://www.federalreserve.gov

US Department of the Treasury
https://www.home.treasury.gov

Referenced Credit Unions
https://www.americaschristiancu.com
https://catholicunitedcu.org
https://www.thriventcu.com

Chapter 5

Balancing Your Checkbook

"I can't be overdrawn—I still have checks!" That seems funny, until the laugh is on you. If an NSF seems to come out of the blue, then either your bookkeeping skills are sloppy, or the bank made a mistake. Most often, it's a case of juggling too many due dates with too few dollars, which makes an NSF no surprise at all.

When I bounced a check, I would wonder to myself, *What's the problem, dummy? Keeping an accurate balance is nothing more than applying elementary math to recorded transactions.* Nevertheless, if we regard ourselves as smarter than a fifth-grader, why can't we accomplish something as simple as tying our shoes? It's because, as humans, we occasionally create an unintentional error or depend solely on our brain for addition and subtraction. Quite rarely will the bank do the former—and positively never does the latter.

It is important to perform a bank reconciliation each month, to ensure that you and the bank stay on the same page. In this chapter, you'll learn sightless use of a calculator and error-tracing techniques for your register. With both skills, you'll be smarter than those sitting in the lobby, waiting for a bank rep to help them straighten out their balance.

Manipulating a Calculator

The hunt-and-peck method of entering digits into a calculator increases the likelihood of unintended consequences—as do typing and texting goofs. Adding machines and printing calculators are manufactured for use with the right hand, so southpaws will have more trouble developing dexterity. The cost of these essential tools is incidental. Buy an accounting calculator, which comes with plenty of features—especially a tape.

The following tutorial will minimize register-balance mistakes: Begin in the neutral position, by placing your middle finger lightly on the calculator's number "5." It has a tactile bump for sightless reference—as do the "f" and "j" on a keyboard. Your index finger should touch "4," and your ring finger should hover slightly over the "6." Push and release any one of these three keys to enter (as if you didn't already know). To choose "1," drop your index finger one row. For "2," drop your middle finger by the same amount. Do likewise with your ring finger for "3." In each case, return to the neutral position after you've performed the function. By now, you've guessed that you strike "7," "8," and "9" with your index, middle, and ring fingers by moving up one row. For zero, which customarily sits below the "1," use your right thumb. To enter a decimal point, drop your ring finger two rows to find it. There's no need to enter a comma—it's built into the programming. For addition or subtraction, first push and release the desired integer, and train your pinkie to find the plus or minus button. To reach a subtotal, find the button that resembles this shape: <>. Striking the * key always ends the calculation string and gives you its total. For either point of reference, train whichever finger you want to achieve that objective.

You can develop quick, mindless accuracy by creating a list of random values and entering them repeatedly without looking at the machine. When the total results are the same time after time, you've mastered the skill. As with keyboarding, you'll use it the rest of your life. I don't know how girls with long nails do it so well, but you do! That covers the basics. Read your owner's manual to learn about your new machine's many features.

Performing a Bank Reconciliation

Gather your current deposit receipts and open up your latest statement. You will find pages inside that chronicle your month's account activity, but probably not your canceled checks. Banks now commonly image them on a statement page to save postage. If you ever need a canceled check for proof of payment, the bank is obligated to provide you with a free copy of both sides. An exception is that of an ACH item. Recall that a clearing-house shredded your check after converting it into an electronic-payment request. Obviously, the bank can't image what it never received back. Proof of payment must come from your reconciled bank statement and register; that's one reason to file them.

Balancing per Bank

Balancing per bank is a reconciliation method that works from the assumption that the bank is correct—and normally is so. Banks may, or may not, include a worksheet with your statement to do the math required to bring the two balances into agreement. In case your bank doesn't supply one, I've illustrated a typical format in figure 5-1 and included it as a tear-out in the back.

Step A asks for your statement's ending balance. You'll find it both in the activity summary and at the end of your transaction history. Step B calls for adding all outstanding deposits or other credits that don't appear on your statement. Step C is the addition of A and B. Step D requires totaling all outstanding checks, withdrawals, and other debits that don't appear this month. Now, subtract step D's total from C's total. The remainder, whether positive or negative, should match the balance in your register. If the two balances don't match, errors must be traced before you know how much money you have left.

If the above procedure is no clearer than mud, let's resolve any questions by examining the details of each step as I teach you an alternative

Worksheet to balance your account

Follow the steps below to reconcile your statement balance with your account register balance. Be sure that your register shows any interest paid into your account and any service charges, automatic payments or ATM transactions withdrawn from your account during this statement period.

[A] **Enter the ending balance** on this statement. $ _____|_____

[B] **List outstanding deposits and other credits** to your account that do not appear on this statement. **Enter the total** in the column to the right.

Description	Amount
Total $		

▶ + $ _____|_____

[C] Add [A] and [B] to calculate the subtotal.   = $ _____|_____

[D] **List outstanding checks, withdrawals, and other debits** to your account that do not appear on this statement. **Enter the total** in the column to the right.

Number/Description	Amount
Total $		

▶ - $ _____|_____

[E] Subtract [D] from [C] to calculate the adjusted ending balance. This amount should be the same as the current balance shown in your register.   = $ _____|_____

Figure 5-1   Worksheet to Balance Your Account

reconciliation method. The exercise will expose mental errors, such as confusing debits and credits, and will locate the missing data confounding your balance.

Balancing per Book

Balancing per book works from the assumption that you are the authority—which might be the case. There is no worksheet. Instead, calculations begin with your register's balance and work backward to prove it against your statement's ending balance. To do a reconciliation using either method, preliminary steps need to be performed; I've listed them in this section to avoid repetition.

Go to your statement's transaction history, where we'll first work on your credit items. Find the first entry's amount, under the Deposits/Additions column, and place a check mark next to it. Its description and posting date are to its left or right, depending on format. Then, move to your checkbook register, locate the corresponding value (usually a deposit) under the credit column, and put a check mark in the narrow adjacent column. If the entry isn't in your register, you've found your first error. You may have neglected to record a paycheck. That often happens with direct deposit, so examine your check stub, and compare dollar amounts. If that's not the mistake, then the issue involves another one of your credits. Your statement gives you a description of what it represents. Find it among your receipts and record it. It could be interest added by the bank or funds that were transferred from your savings account or, perhaps, from a guardian's account. Continue down the page until each and every credit item has been marked off the statement and similarly marked in your register.

Afterward, you can move to your deductions, withdrawals, and subtractions, which, again, are your debit items. Go to the first item under your statement's Withdrawals/Subtractions column. If that's a numbered check, it will be described. Place a check mark beside it. Proceed to your register, find the corresponding check, and mark it off—using that narrow column. Return to the statement for the next entry. If it's another numbered check, repeat as above. If it isn't a check, then it's one of these debit items:

- Check-printing charge
- Monthly maintenance fee
- EFT (Electronic Funds Transfer)
- BA (Bank Authorization) or AP (automatic payment)
- Debit-card payment
- ATM charge
- NSF fee
- Transfer out of your account (by wire or withdrawal slip)
- Any other type of withdrawal that's not listed (the description will be to its left)

Any deduction not in your register scores as an error. Record it now on one of those blank lines you were encouraged to leave between monthly activities. If you forgot, you have no choice but to use the next available line—which may be two pages away. That will make reconciling really cumbersome, buddy.

Continue down the statement until you check off each debit item, and similarly mark your register. At that point, draw a pencil line across your register under the final checked item—debit or credit, as in figure 5-2. This is your cutoff point, and you shouldn't have to deal with anything below it until next month's reconciliation. Now you must strike a balance and place it on that pencil line. This **trial balance** will show if your figure equals your bank statement's ending balance.

You start the tape at your register's last-known **proven balance**. This is the spot in your register where you last ended a successful reconciliation. In other words, you were satisfied that your records matched the bank's version; everything was hunky dory. If you're working with your very first statement, your last-known proven balance will be zero because you began with a blank slate. (Hint: When I establish any proven

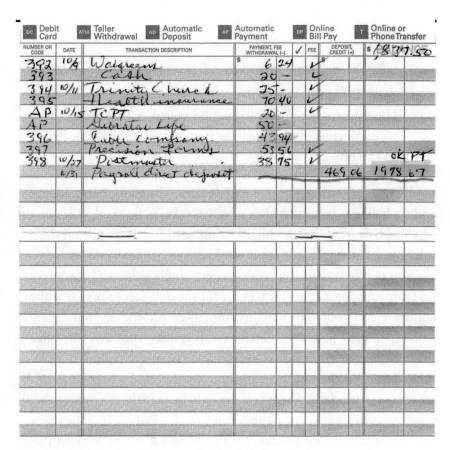

Figure 5-2 Reconciled Register. (Courtesy of Deluxe Checks.)

balance, I highlight it in yellow and initial it. This way I know where to resume next time, and know that everything above it is correct.)

The Trial Balance

As above, the **trial balance** is your initial arithmetic attempt to see if your register reflects the bank's statement.

1. Enter the last-known proven balance into your calculator. (Remembering to first hit the total button twice or more to clear it.)

2. Add to it all credits—checked off or not—down to the line you just drew.

3. Subtract all debits—checked off or not—again, down through that cutoff line.

4. Hit the total for your balance and pencil-in that sum atop your register's cutoff line. Negative amounts go in brackets, like this: <$150.68>.

In the event that the penciled balance matches your statement's ending balance, breathe a sigh of relief—you're finished. Rewrite the penciled balance in ink, highlight it, and initial it. Just to be on the safe side, run a tape again—as many bookkeepers habitually do.

You will have had to mark off every single debit and credit entry on both your statement and register for the balances to match without adjustment. If but one remains unmarked on either, your balances won't (and can't possibly) match, which is often the case. Most likely, the issue here is timing—the bank doesn't have a clue about checks or other debits on the way, or it may not have posted a deposit as of the statement print date, which is a **deposit-in-transit**. Any checks written during the statement period, but not checked off in your register, are your **outstanding checks**. Dab these and deposits-in-transit with a yellow highlighter. Do the same with any withdrawal not checked. This trick will help you locate them during this and possibly the next reconciliation.

To adjust for these timing issues, *add* your outstanding checks *to* that pencil balance in your register and *subtract* your deposits-in-transit *from* it. This should make your two balances match (if they were the only problems). You are done, and can ink, highlight, and initial your register's penciled balance. This becomes your latest-proven balance. If you're still off, recheck your math. This is when a tape helps—you can visibly compare your work with the register. If you're satisfied that the numbers are right, but still have a pesky difference, roll up your sleeves a little higher.

Making Adjustments and Tracing Errors

Dyslexic transcription is common to me. I've written a check for $49.32 and registered it as $39.42. I would have caught that error if I had paid close attention to debit item amounts when marking off canceled checks. I didn't, and was off by $9.90. Your math teacher will tell you that if the amount you're off by comes out to a whole number after dividing by nine, chances are quite high that you've transposed numerals.

Knowing the disposition of every check in your pad and its corresponding register entry is essential as well. For instance, you'll occasionally mess up a check while writing it. Don't scratch out the original register entry—that can knock off your balance. It also makes auditors go nuts. Worse yet, don't try to make a correction and mail the check. Banks suspect fraud when they see chicken scratching, and won't honor the item. If that happens, one of the parties to the check may end up paying a charge. Shred your mistake and write a fresh check. And, because you were supposed to have recorded the goofed-up check in your register before writing it, you'll have to make a reversing entry there to cancel the flub. To make a **reversing entry**, write "To void check number such and such" on a new register line and enter the check's dollar amount in brackets—like this: <$20>.

The same holds true if you write a check and decide not to send it. If you need to reverse a deposit or another credit item, you would similarly write a description and put the amount in brackets in the credit column. Just remember to hit the plus button for debit-entry reversals and the minus button for credit reversals when you come to these items, while trying to strike a balance below them.

A less common correction is that of reversing a stale date check. You want some disposition of it because tracking one becomes unwieldy if you have to flip way back or locate previous registers to work with it. Make life easier by going back to the said party and inquiring about the check's status. Maybe it's still in a desk drawer. Maybe the dog actually ate it, and the payee is embarrassed to tell you. Work things out. If Marge wants a replacement, make a reversing entry and write her a new one. If the check in question is lost, call a banker and decide on a prudent course of action. Fees associated with a stop-payment action don't make sense when they exceed the check amount.

You may read "Void after ninety days" on a business check. This practice keeps their outstanding-check volume manageable. If you own one that exceeds its validity date, call the issuer for a replacement.

In rare instances, a bank error will cause your inability to balance, and addressing it should be done in a timely fashion. In your statement, you'll find procedures and timelines for reporting bank inaccuracies. The bank will investigate at its own expense, and it may take weeks to recover your missing money. Meanwhile, you won't have use of the disputed funds.

Lastly, you could be off by some small, odd amount—like $2.50— that you just can't seem to trace, and the nasty creature keeps popping up when trying to reconcile three or four statements at one sitting. This error comes from sloppy bookkeeping, but the exasperation of unsuccessfully trying to find it may not be worth the effort. If you're certain you have all of your big ducks in a row, go ahead and make a correcting-register entry. If you don't, it will be back the next month. Accountants, on the other hand, obsess over this. They wonder, "Is this difference the net of a credit and a debit? How could I miss them both?" Believe me, professionals have ways of finding the rascal.

After you've finished balancing, file your statement and any related documentation in your Current Year Bank Statements expandable file jacket. After you file your tax returns, put the twelve in with them and keep everything until you safely dispose of the returns.

In review, you can help maintain an accurate register balance by using an accounting calculator that has a tape and full-size buttons. This practice reduces surprise NSF occurrences. Reconciling your checkbook within a week of receiving your monthly statement will also tell you precisely where you stand.

Chapter 6

❧ ❧

GETTING A GRIP ON TAXES

An Overview on Taxes

We have charged the public sector with building the roads and bridges that connect us, and with supplying the fresh water that hydrates us. Its assignments are nothing new. The Appian Way and the Roman aqueducts stood in place when our Savior walked the earth. Then, just as now, public levies paid for such projects. Our Lord's once-tax-collector Matthew could surely tell us stories about resistance to this imposition, which hasn't stopped two millennia later. In point, British taxes were a flash point for the American Revolution.

In forming US tax code, the Founding Fathers shared the philosophy that, before you must begin paying tax on earnings, you can exclude a portion of what it takes to feed and clothe yourself and get a roof over your head. Accordingly, they created the **personal exemption** and the **standard deduction** as income offsets. The 2017 Congress modified this safety net for 2018 as part of the Tax Cuts and Jobs Act of 2017 (TCJA). It eliminated the personal exemption, for the time being, and dramatically raised the standard deduction to the point that it eclipsed the sum of the former two. According to Internal Revenue Bulletin (IRB): 2018–10, the standard deduction for a single person in 2018 was $12,000. It's expected this number will rise in the coming years. Decision makers will base changes in income thresholds, deduction amounts, and credit values based on what happens with the Chained Consumer Price Index (C-CPI). In 2025, tax law is due to change again.

Tax postponement and tax avoidance remain a part of US tax code. Both strategies are legal—if not prudent—and you'll learn more about them here. These differ from tax evasion, which can result in prison time.

> Anyone may arrange his affairs so that his taxes shall be as low as possible; he is not bound to choose that pattern which best pays the treasury. There is not even a patriotic duty to increase one's taxes. Over and over again the Courts have said that there is nothing sinister in so arranging affairs as to keep taxes as low as possible. Everyone does it, rich and poor alike and all do right, for nobody owes any public duty to pay more than the law demands.
>
> —Judge Learned Hand, *Helvering v. Gregory*,
> 69 F.2d 809, 810 (2d Cir. 1934),
> aff'd, 293 U.S. 465 (1935)

There's been progress on the moral front, as well. Centuries ago, people went to debtors' prison for inability to pay what they owed, and their children had to work to earn the "ransom money." Contemporary bankruptcy law precludes this scenario, although individuals still face confinement if the issue involves criminal activity. To top things off, our Constitution guarantees freedom of speech, which allows you to express your opinion to legislators who have the authority to change the rules. Vote the bums out if you're still not happy.

In this chapter, you'll learn when you must file your first tax return; have our cardinal tax terms defined; and be introduced to ways for reducing your taxes. I may even be able to help you get some money back. Finally, we'll view the tax return of a gal who isn't far ahead of you.

In practice, as soon as the first dollar is withheld from your check, you've paid taxes. Filing an annual return is simply the arithmetic exercise that squares you up with the IRS. The 1040's bottom line indicates whether you're due a refund or need to pay more.

Let's look at where it all starts.

IRS Form W-4

On orientation day at work, you're required to complete an **IRS Form W-4** to set up your federal and state withholding. An important line in its Personal Allowances Worksheet asks if you are a **head of household**, which carries with it a higher standard deduction and better tax rates.

"I'm the ranking roommate. Do I qualify?" I'm afraid not. A head of household is an unmarried person who provides the major support of a qualified parent or related person, such as old Aunt Betsy.

If you're legally blind, your standard deduction will rise by another $1,600. Those who are married, or have dependents, qualify for more allowances. In all cases, read and follow the W-4 instructions.

The takeaway is that an increasing number of allowances lowers the amount of taxes withheld—which makes for a fatter check on payday. Claiming zero on the W-4 results in less take-home pay than does the standard "1" for single people, but it could make for a healthier refund. It's almost like having a savings account. Furthermore, you can stipulate an additional flat amount withheld to push the total higher, by asking your employer to do so.

Who Must File, and at What Age?

At first, you would think that a five-year-old doesn't have to pay taxes or file a tax return. Well, if she's a child actress on a popular sitcom, you'd better believe that Congress has fashioned laws to funnel some of her plentiful earnings to the US Treasury. The law reads, in essence, that you're subject to the income-tax system on the day you earn your first dollar. Official filing requirements are in the **IRS Form 1040** instructions and on the IRS website, where you can download that and other forms, along with corresponding instructions; basic forms are generally available at the library as well. In addition, the website holds a wealth of user information. Tabs bring you to pages that proactively address questions that students and others commonly ask.

To uninitiated readers, I'll give you the *Reader's Digest* version concerning filing. The obligation to file hinges on tests of how much money you've earned and where it came from. In its general filing requirements, the IRS says if you have earned income that exceeds the standard deduction, you must file a federal tax return—again, regardless of age. **Earned income** includes wages, tips, salaries, and taxable scholarship and fellowship grants. Another test concerns unearned income. **Unearned income** is primarily interest on bank accounts and dividends from investments. Current IRS publications will tell you how much of it is exempt before it becomes an issue. Lastly, there is a group of miscellaneous filing requirements, most of which pertain to self-employed people. With that said, those of you with income this year fall into one of two groups, which I label "A" and "B."

Group A: Above the Standard Deduction

If you earned more than the standard deduction this year, you are in group A, and must file a return. Next January, your employer will give you the multipart **IRS Form W-2**, which shows how your total payroll dollars were distributed. One part is to be included with your federal return, and another accompanies your state return, unless you're lucky enough to live in states that have no income taxes. (The last W-2 copy is for your records.) All things being equal, you'll be entitled to a refund if you filled out your W-4 correctly, because your employer will have withheld more than enough money. If you're paid under the table in cash, you won't receive a W-2, but are still required to "render unto Caesar." In this case, you must file the 1040 long form—along with an **IRS Schedule SE** (Self-Employment tax, Social Security, and Medicare contributions)—if you earn more, in total, than the standard deduction.

Check with your folks before you file a tax return. They may still be claiming you as a dependent, thus utilizing your allowance.

Group B: Below the Standard Deduction

You are in Group B if you earned money at jobs during the current tax year, but your total is lower than the standard deduction. You don't have to file a return. Doing so will be a wash, and the IRS figures doing so just wastes everybody's time. So, go ahead and temporarily exhale a sigh of relief.

However, you may still want to file a return. Why? Because that's the only way to obtain a refund of any taxes that were withheld. Millions of refundable dollars remain unclaimed because people don't know better or are tentative about filing. To quote the IRS website: *Even if you do not have to file a return, you should file one to get a refund of any Federal Income Tax withheld.*

The same holds true to receive a refund of taxes withheld at an old part-time job for which you've never filed a return. If that's so, file the tax return for that year and rightfully claim your refund. Cool. The IRS archives the old forms, and I have included the necessary IRS ULR page at the end of this chapter. Your time limit is three years.

You will need to file **IRS Form 1040X** to correct a mistake on a return for a previous year. This is known as **amending a tax return**. Incidentally, Social Security and Medicare taxes aren't refundable for either group. Rather, they build up in your account for future use.

Tax Terms

Before we look at a model return, I'll clarify some tax terms and define tax reducers.

Tax Credits

Tax credits are bonuses that directly reduce your tax bill. For example, if you owed $4,000 in taxes, and you qualified for a credit of $500, then your bill is reduced to $3,500. Politicians create tax credits to influence behavior. For instance, Congress has offered a tax credit to businesses for hiring additional employees during recessionary times. Again, if policy-makers want the country to use less energy, they'll give tax credits to people who buy fuel-efficient cars, appliances, and building products. Other tax credits were created to assist low-income individuals and families. The **earned income tax credit** (**EITC**) is a permanent and important one that may someday apply to you. To qualify, you must earn less than a certain amount and file a return. Even if you owe zero in taxes, you might qualify for a payment. See the link at the end of this chapter.

Future administrations will have different goals and will create unique tax credits. Expect Congress to turn incentives on and off as you do a faucet.

Tax-Deductible Items

A **tax-deductible item** is a personal expense that Congress has decided to include on its list of costs that reduce your taxable income. As of this writing, examples include medical and dental expenses; prescription drugs; health-insurance premiums; eyeglasses and contacts; mortgage-loan interest; and more. Rulemakers in DC approximated an average mix of the above particulars to settle on the standard deduction. If your qualifying expenses exceed its dollar limit, you can claim that excess by filing the long form—or **itemizing**, as they call it. Your current list, and any limits, are in the instructions for filing the long form 1040.

Again, the content of these deductions is sure to change, as contemporary administrations struggle to reduce our country's crushing level of debt. Legislators will take back on occasion some of what was previously deductible by reclassifying it or by changing its definition, despite the fact Shakespeare said a rose by any other name is still a rose. For instance, the old, deductible per-gallon gasoline tax is now called an excise tax or user's fee, neither of which is deductible. The same holds true on the federal and state level for "**sin taxes**" on tobacco, marijuana, and alcohol. These **excise taxes** are virtual **windfall profits** for taxing authorities. And view **state lottery games** for exactly what they are—though disguised as entertainment that can have a payout, they are nothing more than voluntary tax contributions.

Tax-Qualified Items

Tax-qualified items are referred to as such because they "qualify" for special tax treatment. Contributions to your savings plans at work (401k, et al.) and your individual retirement account (IRA) make up the bulk of tax-qualified items.

Tax-Deferred and Tax-Exempt Status

Items that gain **tax-deferred status** are profit dollars inside certain investment arrangements. The IRS says that if you enter into such, it will wait until you take your money out before collecting any applicable tax. Examples include earnings on the cash value of life insurance policies, annuities, and profits inside tax-qualified savings plans, all of which are covered in Chapters 7 and 10.

Congress has moved some of your purchases into a **tax-exempt status**, in another bid to influence spending. The municipal bond tops the list. Its interest is excluded on your federal return and is exempt for residents of the state that issued it. Also, twenty-nine types of organizations can have their income exempted under section **501(c)** of Title 26 in our tax code. Certain nonprofits—such as churches, private schools, and charitable organizations—can petition the IRS for a designation of **501(c)(3)** Upon approval, your donation qualifies as tax-exempt income for that organization, and you can claim it as a deductible expense.

Filing a Tax Return

The **IRS Form 1040**, which may include supplemental schedules, is known as the **long form**. A simple return is known as the **short form**, which the IRS has currently labeled as the 1040EZ. The decision to file long or short should be based upon the dollar total of your tax-deductible items. File the **IRS Form EZ** if you don't have any tax-deductible expenses, or very few in dollar amount.

Methods of filing your IRS Form 1040 have changed over the years. Decades ago, taxpayers worked from a booklet the IRS mailed. Later on, they could file simple returns telephonically. Now, in the digital age, people can file online, but mailing a hard copy is still an accepted method. You can file one yourself, utilize an online service, or take your documents to a professional tax preparer. In addition, the IRS website can connect you with a dozen or so cost-free preparation services, as long as you meet the criteria. No matter which filing method you choose, it's up to you to save your documentation, along with a copy of your return. To be on the safe side, keep it for seven years. It won't take up much space.

Federal and state returns are due April 15—which, by coincidence, isn't long after April Fool's Day. The deadline is extended when April 15 falls on Saturday, Sunday, or a federal holiday. If you are required to file, owe taxes, and miss the cutoff, you'll have to pay interest on any money owed when you finally do file.

The IRS does realize that extenuating circumstances can preclude you from filing on time. Besides procrastination, any number of things could go wrong. You might be deathly sick, records could be lost—or maybe you are in a combat zone. Relax, the IRS isn't going to hold your feet to the fire. By law, you are entitled to an automatic four-month filing extension. You must notify the IRS of your intention by completing **IRS Form 4868**, and filing it by April 15, as you would your tax return. Your tax preparer can do it for you as well. I want to make it clear that Form 4868 *is not an extension to pay what you owe*. It only gives you extra time to file. If you believe that more money will be due, pay it by the deadline above to avoid a penalty. This can be done by credit card or EFT at the IRS website. Phone your local IRS office if you can't come up with the funds, and someone will gladly set up a payment program for you.

A Teen's Model Tax Return

We're far enough along now to put the above concepts on paper. Instead of illustrating a young lady's example on the ever-changing 1040 format,

I streamlined her work flow in a vertical equation to better illustrate the progression. Our friend Alexis shares an apartment, which keeps her living expenses low. She probably doesn't dine out much, and may have patches on her jeans. I don't know, but Alexis' annual budget allows her to contribute $1,500 annually into her tax-qualified retirement plan at work and to invest $1,200 in her IRA (both of which we'll cover in Chapter 10). Additionally, she has an interest-bearing savings account and inherited a tax-exempt bond. She earned $28,500 at her job, which puts her in the 12 percent tax bracket. Her employer withheld $3,100 for federal taxes. As a bonus, she can take advantage of a $200 tax credit. Figure 6-1 shows how things go arithmetically.

Income	
Gross earning at work	$28,500
Subtract plan contributions	–1,500
Reportable W-2 earnings	$27,000
Bond interest	($475)
Add her savings account interest	50
Total taxable income	$27,050
Adjustments	
Subtract IRA contribution	–1,200
Adjusted gross income	$25,850
Subtract the 2018 standard deduction	–12,000
Adjusted taxable income:	$13,650
Tax on $13,650 (from 1040 instructions)	$1,447
Subtract the tax credit	200
Tax liability	$1,247
Tax withheld	$3,100
Refund due	$1,853

Figure 6-1   Alexis' 2018 Tax Return

A closer look at our pal's return shows that both her IRA and work-plan contributions simultaneously reduced her taxable income and her increased assets. The tax-exempt bond interest won't count toward her total income but will be listed on the return, because the issuer reports it to the IRS by name and Social Security number, and Uncle Sam will look for a match.

Alexis's tax is not a flat 12 percent of $13,650 because of her **marginal tax rate**. As of 2018, individuals are taxed at the rate of only 10 percent on their first $9,525. In calculating her bill, that would be $952, so far. Amounts over $9,525, but less than $38,700, are taxed at 12 percent. Therefore, her next $4,125 of earnings ($13,650 minus $9,525) are taxed at 12 percent, which adds another $495 and gives a grand total of $1,447. (Tax brackets and tax tables for the current year are at irs.gov.) The amount of tax withheld depended on how Alexis filled out her W-4. If she wants to change things, she may complete a new one.

Alexis received her refund the fast way: By providing her bank account routing and checking numbers on the return, it arrived at her bank by EFT.

Not everyone feels confident about filing his or her first tax return. The anguish some filers experience stems more often from a fear of completing the form incorrectly, rather than from the dread of having to pay more money. If you make a mistake, the IRS won't put you in jail. An agent will simply make the correction and send you a letter explaining what was done. If additional tax is due, the IRS correspondence will include remittance options. Then again, errors can fall in your favor. However, it is worth noting that an IRS agent, such as above, will never, ever telephone you; he or she will always contact you via mail. Any caller posing as an IRS agent is a scammer. Hang up and call the police.

Final Considerations

To conclude, I want to add an important word about hiring on with a company that gives the impression that you're an employee but, instead, treats you like an independent contractor.

First of all, let's define that term. An **independent contractor** is in business for himself or herself, and contracts out his or her often-specialized product or service to more than one company or individuals. This arrangement works well for company X that, for example, wants to publish just an in-house operations manual. It might then contract with a writer and a **freelance** (again, not on someone's payroll) photographer and take the assembled text and pictures to a printing company to bind it all. Then management will have accomplished its objective without having to add a writer and photographer—who won't have anything to do anymore—onto the payroll. Instead, the writer and photographer will go forth with checks in hand, searching for their next opportunity.

At the end of the calendar year, company X will send the writer and photographer each an **IRS Form 1099**, which shows how much they were paid for their services. Company X will also send the identical information to the IRS. Our two independent contractors will then have to file a 1040 long form—complete with self-employment supplemental schedule (IRS Form SE)—and pay their own Social Security and Medicare tax, as well as having to match it. That could amount to an additional 15.3 percent of their earnings paid in taxes. The two must also estimate their annual income and send the IRS the applicable tax on a quarterly basis. And any state tax liability will go on top of that. Moreover, our two independent contractors won't be receiving any company benefits, such as 401(k) money or health insurance coverage.

Other examples of independent contractors are beauticians, barbers, real estate agents, and sales professionals who represent a number of companies' products.

So, if you're "hired" to go door to door selling nothing but the latest fandango, inquire ahead of time to see if you'll be receiving payroll checks through the month and a W-2 at the end of the year. If not, the so-called employer may just be trying to avoid the cost of matching Social Security and Medicare taxes by calling you an independent contractor. I've provided an IRS link covering independent contractors or employees, to help you learn more about the determination.

I expect that you'll be getting exposure to pyramid and Ponzi schemes too. They're illegal—just ask or do a search on "Bernie Madoff." That isn't to say there aren't reputable **multi-level marketing companies**, which may resemble pyramid companies but operate above board. The Federal Trade Commission (FTC) and your state's department of commerce can help you with information about current schemes and honest companies.

And lastly, any time you contact the IRS on the Web, be absolutely positive that you've typed in the correct URL. Imposter sites with very similar addresses are waiting to steal your identity.

Many happy returns.

Helpful Links

Internal Revenue Service

https://www.irs.gov

https://www.irs.gov/forms-pubs/prior-year

https://www.irs.gov/businesses/small-businesses-self-employed/independent-contractor-self-employed-or-employee

Information on the earned income tax credit (EITC)

https://www.irs.gov/credits-deductions/individuals/earned-income-tax-credit

Chapter 7

Managing Life's Risks through Insurance

Our stay on earth is punctuated by periods of injury and sickness, and it may end when we least expect it. Along the way, we can use insurance companies to help finance us through difficult financial times. But that's not an earth-shattering statement; any classmate can tell you that insurance is about as self-explanatory as a hammer. Be that as it may, I couldn't get my head around certain aspects of life insurance as a high school freshman. I remember wondering, *If we both know I'm going to die, then why do insurance companies bet that I won't? I could rake in the cash by proving them wrong!* With that dumb logic, I'd have to die to prove I was right. As you'll read, it turns out I was closer to the truth than I thought.

I bought a life policy after high school because Dad made me. I took it on faith the decision would serve me later, but remained confused about how the math worked when looking at its cash-value projections and how the contract would benefit me while living. Enlightenment had to wait until I earned my insurance credentials. Today, I'll share that information and tell you some secrets. Then you'll have all you need to make good decisions without having to take an insurance certification course.

I know you're not clueless. A student once told me, "You buy car insurance for the same reason you do life insurance. If you total your $15,000 SUV, you won't suffer a financial loss, just as your folks won't if you're unlucky enough to die in the crash. After all, the undertaker will want as much to make you look pretty again and get you in the ground."

This guy knew the elements of **risk management**, and may have gone on to become a master statistician or an **actuary**—or maybe a bookie, if the character went down the wrong path. In all cases, a good risk manager recognizes the probable and the inevitable and opts to shift the unaffordable percentage of the applicable financial risks to the insurance company. How much is an unaffordable percentage? You base that decision on your level of cash reserves and the value of your non-essential assets. The wealthier you are, the more **self-insured** you are. Other choices play out as sad stories in the news, such as keeping fingers crossed that generous strangers will donate at gofundme.com.

As you'll see in Chapter 12, the cost of managing risk can actually be a fairly small percentage of your budget. But to continue, let's read about one of your friends who found he had something you might own, but don't yet know.

Life Insurance

Whole Life Policies

Joshua recently turned nineteen, when his dad handed him a manila envelope with an old postmark. He was surprised to see that it was his life insurance policy. Josh wondered aloud, "What's this?"

"It's a $10,000 policy Mom and I bought for you when you were in diapers. It's called a **juvenile policy**. Take a look. The **declaration page** says that you are both the owner and the insured. Mom and I are **beneficiaries**. Now that you're of age, you assume its control and can make any changes you want."

"Why did you guys buy this? Was I a sickly kid? Did you think I was going to die?" Josh worried.

"No, son," his dad chuckled. "I think that was pretty far from our minds. Parents cover that risk by adding a **family rider** to their own life policy. Actually, we were thinking of your future. This **whole life**

policy is permanent protection that can't be taken away. The overriding motivation for buying it was that it gives you at least some insurance in adulthood should you ever contract a life-threatening disease. That could make you **uninsurable**. We could have selected a higher amount, but nothing over the top. Reputable companies won't insure a baby's life for a fortune. On the other hand, if you turned out to be a child piano prodigy, we could have called Lloyd's of London or some company like that to **underwrite** your talented little fingers in an effort to protect your earning power."

"How much are the premiums, Dad? I want to keep this thing going."

"It's paid up," his dad answered. "The term '**whole life**' doesn't mean that you have to pay premiums until the day you die. It means the policy covers the span of your life. By contrast, a **term life policy** affords coverage for only a specific number of years.

"Whole-life premiums are set for a fixed amount, based upon your age and gender, and will never go up. Juvenile policy rates are among the lowest because of the company's negligible risk of insuring a healthy infant, and are typically designed to be fully funded in twenty years. Yours began running on automatic pilot because the premiums and interest built enough cash value to carry itself. Not only that, but the company paid us **dividends**, which reflect a return of company profits to policyholders. (Insurance companies that pay dividends are known as **participating** companies. Those that don't are categorized as **nonparticipating**.) Mom and I elected to have these dollars automatically buy **paid-up insurance**, which ultimately increased your policy's death benefit."

His dad went on to explain that a policy's **face amount** is its stated level of coverage, but the **death benefit** payable could be higher—as above—or lower because of any outstanding loan.

"Gee, Pop, what should I do with my policy?"

"If I were you, I'd set an appointment with Mark Jackson, our insurance agent, to hear what he has to say."

Joshua did just that. We pick up on Joshua and Mark's conversation, after their greetings:

"Your parents' small, thoughtful gift has grown to become a valuable asset," Mark observed.

"Yes, I'm impressed. Can I buy a policy for another person, like my folks did for me?" Josh asked.

"You can if you have an **insurable interest** in that party," Mark explained. "In other words, you would have to prove a financial hardship on your part if the insured died.

"You said that you had some interest in knowing what options you have for your policy," he continued. "For one thing, you can just leave it alone. Another is to **surrender** it for cash. If you do, you're going to pay a good share of the proceeds in taxes and leave yourself uninsured. As long as earnings remain inside a policy, the IRS considers the profit tax-deferred. If you terminate a policy early, interest becomes taxable income. However, both contributions and interest go to your beneficiary tax-free when you die. Not only that, if you surrender or exchange a policy, the original insurance company is off the hook. They won that bet and made a clear profit.

"One choice is to put it in with a new larger, flexible permanent policy, which can both serve as an investment while you're single and protect your family if you marry. The generic name for this now-industry-standard is **flexible premium adjustable whole life**—better known as **universal life,** or simply, **UL.**

"A UL policy comes with a stated rate of return and contains a **table of guaranteed value**. That page tells you what your policy will be worth each year. But if a policy is issued during a period of very low interest rates," Mark cautioned, "it's not likely to perform well as an investment over the long run. Accordingly, some investment advisors suggest that you 'buy term (insurance) and invest the rest.' The 'rest' is the premium difference between term and whole life for the same face amount of coverage. For example, the premium for a cash-value whole life policy may be five times higher than for comparable term coverage—with age being the most influential factor.

"To remain competitive, and to provide value for policyholders, insurance companies developed **variable universal life (VUL)**," Mark added. "In such, your premiums are invested in mutual funds [stock and bond packages are covered in Chapter 9], thereby offering an opportunity for a higher rate of return. But mutual funds operate within the stock market, and if it tanks in a policy's early years, there's a real possibility that you will have to dump in money to keep your VUL from lapsing. VUL is appropriate for people willing to assume some risk with their cash value, but not recommended for people with a low risk tolerance and marginal net worth.

"The younger you are when buying a policy, the cheaper your premiums are going to be," Mark advised. "If you wait until you develop health complications like, say, diabetes or heart problems, you may still be insurable, but companies will charge more. They call these **rated policies**. Insurance company actuaries use a **mortality table**—which predicts how long you'll live—and consider other factors when setting rates and deciding whether or not to **underwrite** you (issue you a policy). Once that's done, companies can't back out of this contract or raise your rates if you get sick. It's then said to be a **noncancelable policy**. However, if you don't pay your premiums, your policy will **lapse.**

"Lifestyles do make a difference, Josh. I've witnessed an occasion when a company declined coverage after an applicant checked 'yes' on an application for using drugs. Had he lied about his history and landed coverage, the company would have been off the hook if he overdosed. But after a number of years stated in a policy, the contract is then said to be **incontestable**, and some circumstances can be covered. Some companies will decline coverage to otherwise healthy people if they skydive, or travel to unstable countries," Mark stressed. "Because you're young and healthy, and don't smoke, your premiums are going to be low for a modern policy with coverage that's higher than what you have now.

"Jumpstarting a new policy with the cash value in your juvenile policy really sends future premiums down the steps because large chunks of money at a policy's inception lowers the insurer's risk.

"But never cancel your existing policy and ask for a check to fund a new policy! Doing so is known as taking **constructive receipt** of your money, which makes any policy earnings taxable. Instead, Company A and Company B can swap your cash value in what's known as an **IRS Section 1035 Exchange**. This arrangement is tax-free, and any insurance agent has the application form. If you're considering an exchange, work with a reputable agent," Mark cautioned Josh. "The new policy may not be in your best interest.

"This idea of front-loading a permanent policy is also the basis of **single pay life**. That's another choice," Mark noted. "People who choose it put in a lump sum on day one and never ever have to add another buck. A young person can buy a big policy for very little money. A gift or windfall would work."

"I've heard of an endowment policy, Mr. Jackson. What's that?" Josh asked.

"An **endowment policy** is a contract that ends in ten or twenty years, typically. It's said to **mature** at that time," the agent explained.

"Oh, yeah! I remember drawing a Monopoly card that said my life insurance matured. I bought a hotel with that windfall," Josh chuckled.

"Good move, young man. Let me suggest another: Exchange your juvenile policy for a UL with a higher face. That will permanently insure your income stream if and when you become a breadwinner. That's the whole idea. Burial costs are tiny, compared with what it takes to house, feed, and educate the little ones for ten years or more. Now you're talking about a policy with a face amount in the high six digits, Josh, and I can offer you one with a company that has a AAA rating, which reflects its financial strength and integrity."

"Wow! How can anybody afford a $700,000 policy, or even more, Mr. Jackson?"

"If kids come along, you'll have to decide how much risk you want to take and how much of it you want to transfer to the insurance company. Even if you could afford the right-sized jumbo, smart risk managers advise that you don't restrict yourself to one policy.

"The **master strategy of family protection** model says to start with an adequate, affordable UL policy, then add less expensive term insurance to reach your target. A portion of that may be group coverage that's provided as a benefit at work, with some compensation packages allowing you purchase even more. Group insurance of all types is cheaper because the insurer's claims exposure is spread over millions of employees at various companies across the country.

"Whether you put in a lump sum or not, a UL's flexibility allows for changing circumstances. As your kids grow up, start dropping term coverage. By the time they're all out of the house, adjust down your UL coverage as well.

"And, as the generic-policy description implies, UL premium payments aren't chiseled in stone. This feature lets you send in a higher or lower payment. In fact, you can skip premiums, if you had to. As long as there's sufficient cash value in the policy, the insurer dips into the bucket and takes out enough to make your payment. You can also borrow from your UL's cash value and repay it later without a tax consequence," Mark noted.

"In late policy years, your cash value can amount to a sizable sum. This is when your insurance company is at lower risk. For instance, if you have a $100,000 policy with a $60,000 cash value, the company is really on the hook for only $40,000. The company will send your beneficiary a check for that $100,000, but $60,000 of it is really your own money."

Term Life Policies

"Mr. Jackson, would you tell me a little more about term insurance?"

"Sure, Josh. Again, term policies afford temporary coverage and have much lower premiums because they don't build cash value. And because term is commonly used during one's healthier middle life it makes it a good bet for the insurance company.

"The shortest term is that of one year. If the insured wants to renew after that, the company will require a new application, and maybe another physical. This meets the need of very few, so most people choose an **annual renewable term** policy. A fifteen-year **ART**, for instance, is a one-year policy that automatically renews fifteen times."

"Would I ever want one like that?" Josh asked.

"Under the right circumstances," Mark surmised. "For example, perhaps Meg and Jerry want to guarantee $40,000 in ten years for their daughter's higher education. With their current assets and life insurance, they have every other goal covered if Jerry dies prematurely. Accordingly, they take out a ten-year $40,000 **decreasing term** policy and simultaneously start socking away $4,000 each year. In year two, the contract drops its coverage to $36,000, and scales back annually by $4,000 until it drops to zero. This two-prong strategy makes sure that they'll always have $40,000 if Jerry is no longer with us.

"Housing lenders use the same product for **private mortgage insurance**, or **PMI**. It is required of buyers with insufficient equity in their homes. Lenders, in this case, feel at risk because homeowners might walk away—having little or nothing to lose if things turn sour.

"And finally, Josh, you can exchange your juvenile policy (or any whole life policy) for an annuity contract—tax free."

"What exactly is that, Mr. Jackson?"

"An **annuity contract**—or simply annuity—is the opposite side of the insurance industry's coin," the independent agent explained. "With an insurance policy, you pay premiums during a period of time and get a lump sum at the end. With an annuity, you start with a lump sum and/or make payments during the **accumulation phase**. In retirement, you receive lifetime checks. That's called the **annuitization phase**. It's the best and intended purpose of an annuity. I wouldn't recommend one for you at your age. You have more important bases to cover," Mark cautioned.

"Thanks so very much, Mr. Jackson. I'll give my choices a lot of thought and get back with you," Josh replied, as he grabbed the door handle. "Dad always says to develop a relationship and do business with professionals in their field, instead of using the Internet. They work hardest for you. because their income depends on repeat business and referrals." The end.

As Josh's agent indicated, an annuity doesn't normally figure into a young person's financial plan. This investment is more suitable for people in their forties and fifties. Be that as it may, more descriptive details follow in this next short section. If you want to skip it, go ahead. You can always return here in years to come.

Annuity Contracts

An insurance company writes two types of annuity contracts that build money. This is an annuity's accumulation phase. A **fixed annuity** both guarantees the value of your investment and the interest rate it pays. An example is a twenty-year annuity at 4 percent. You aren't allowed to add more than the initial sum. This is a one-shot deal.

The second kind is the **variable annuity**. It differs in two ways. First, you have the option of adding dollars at any time; and, second, you have the choice of investing in mutual funds (which are comprised of stocks and bonds) within the annuity. These features make it a **flexible annuity**. Because securities offer no guarantee with regard to safety or return, you can't forecast what your investment will be worth in the future.

Far down the road, you'll want to halt the accumulation phase of either and choose to take payments, instead. This is a contract's annuitization phase. As it begins, something critically important happens: The entire lump sum irreversibly becomes the property of the insurance company! From that point on, the company is bound by contract to begin monthly payments to the you, the **annuitant**, based on your expected lifetime and the value of the contract. If you're still alive after that expected date comes and goes, the company is obligated to keep making payments until you do die. If your name is Methuselah, don't bother to apply.

Payment amounts vary by contract type, too. An **immediate annuity** sends a more-than-ample monthly check but comes with a downside potential: If you die before anticipated, the insurer will keep the balance. Remember, it's now the company's money.

A **period-certain annuity** specifies that payments will span a finite number of years (such as ten or fifteen), and then comes to an end, whether you're alive or not. This option increases the size of your payment. Should you die before the cutoff, the balance will go to your beneficiary.

Married couples often choose a **joint annuity**, which covers the lives of both spouses, but has a lower monthly payment per person than either of the above. Reputable companies include terms that call for a beneficiary designation in the event that both spouses pass on, but still have a remaining account balance.

Be aware that an insurance company may assess what's called a **surrender charge** if you cancel the contract during the accumulation phase of any annuity contract. The IRS may hit you as well; it assesses a 10 percent penalty if you withdraw money before a certain age, which is historically fifty-nine and a half. With this in mind, saving for a goal like a vacation home or higher education is not a suitable purpose for an annuity. Don't let any salesman tell you differently.

With all annuity and life contracts, it's best to do business with an insurance company that enjoys a high rating. The A.M. Best company is a well-known insurance company rating service, with the top rating being AAA. Good independent insurance agents can help you select a company which meets this standard.

Disability Income Insurance

Disability income insurance (DI) is another risk-management tool. It provides cash benefits if you are injured or develop a debilitating illness and aren't able to work because of it. A medical doctor must make that determination. Recovery from any injury may take a while, devouring your cash reserves.

Statistics show that a disability is far likelier to occur than is premature death. In setting premium rates, insurance company actuaries consider what type of work you do and consult **morbidity tables**, which reflect how frequently people get sick or are laid up.

DI offers two **benefit periods**, either short-term or long-term. The one you pick determines how long you'll receive a check. This period can range from a year or less to the rest of your life.

The policy's **waiting period** specifies how much time must elapse before benefits kick in. The industry average is ninety days. Selecting a longer waiting period can lower premiums substantially. You can make this choice if you have plenty of cash reserves and adequate **PTO** (**paid time off**), which may be some combination of federal holidays, vacation time, and what were once called sick days.

Short and long-term DI policies are optional employment benefits. When they are, they're sure to be **group insurance plans**, which again, are inexpensive. The party who pays the premiums depends on the generosity of the employer. In most cases, that's going to be you, and costs are deducted from your check. The good news is that your benefits will be tax-exempt if you ever have to use them. If your employer covers the premiums, benefits will be taxable. In both cases, your benefit checks will be lower by about a third of your normal take-home pay.

In the absence of a policy at work, you bear the wage-loss risk if injury or illness strikes. This possibility becomes more of a factor as you move up the income ladder and are operating a large budget. Some people shop for a personal DI policy to mitigate the risk of having to slash expenses for an extended period. Typically, your DI check will be about 60 percent of your payroll check.

An important consideration when choosing a personal DI policy is what the insurance company has to say about you and your career. A bargain-rate policy may deem that a highly paid master carpenter, now in a wheelchair, can easily work in a call center for peanuts, and will stop paying benefits. A policy that protects job classification and income levels will cost you more in premiums, but will protect your earning power.

Protecting yourself from both the possible and the inevitable is one of the four cornerstones of your financial foundation. Many Christian-denomination insurers, such as the Lutheran Thrivent Financial and the Catholic Knights of Columbus Insurance, offer DI and life policies.

Workers' Compensation

If you get sick because of a working condition or are injured while carrying out your job, your state **workers' compensation program** will cover about two-thirds of your check. This money is not taxable at the state or federal level at the time of this writing.

A worker's compensation program is a form of insurance, which is paid for by employers throughout the state, even though arrangements may be state-funded, administered by an insurance company, or paid out directly. Structures and details vary by your state of residence. In all cases, you're entitled to receive immediate medical attention, and there's no waiting period before benefits begin.

A worker's comp physician calls the shots regarding how long benefits will last. If Dr. Jane says you're now well enough to return to work, that's where you'll go. If Dr. Mike says that you need six weeks of physical therapy beforehand, he'll prescribe it, and workers' comp will pay the bill. Very rarely will you be required to bear a portion of cost, but this possibility could come in the form of an **insurance deductible**.

Social Security Disability Insurance

The **Social Security Disability** program serves as a safety net if you become permanently disabled and have no other source of income. Qualifying is difficult, though, and benefits are taxable. You can apply at a local Social Security office, where folks will help you with details.

Renters Insurance

It's important to understand that a property owner is not legally responsible for the safety or condition of the contents of your dorm room or apartment. If a fire or flood wrecks your stuff, you're out of luck unless you have a **renters insurance policy**. Ten to fifteen dollars per month will get you one, and the insurer will replace your personal property if it's damaged or lost during certain natural disasters, such as tornadoes, earthquakes, and volcanic eruptions. You're also covered if your belongings are consumed by fire, or if stolen. An **extended-coverage** policy provision further protects your property while you're away from home. For example, if someone walks off with your suitcase, your insurance company will reimburse you for it and its contents. The same holds true if someone breaks into your car and steals valuables. Note, however, that you may need to add special coverage for firearms.

As with auto coverage, a renters policy includes a deductible provision, which represents your share of the risk. For instance, if your loss totals $3,782, and you've chosen a five-hundred-dollar deductible, you can expect a check for only $3,282. If you select a higher deductible, your insurance company will lower the annual premium.

Renters insurance doesn't indemnify you against inundation. To cover that situation, buy **federal flood insurance**—the cost of which can be significant for those living in a floodplain. On the other hand, if water backs up from a sewer drain and saturates your belongings with stinky stuff, a standard renters policy covers the bill. In both situations, it may be smarter to choose an apartment on the second floor.

Moreover, a renters policy provides coverage for bodily injury and property damage to others caused by your actions or negligence no matter where you are.

Umbrella Insurance

An **umbrella insurance policy** is a master-coverage policy that picks up at the point where your auto, renters, or homeowner's liability insurance leaves off. It generally starts out with a million dollars in coverage and may have a standard $5,000 deductible. For the sake of illustration: Imagine that you're facing a $600,000 problem, and your primary policy will provide only $300,000 to settle the issue. Your umbrella policy will cover you for the difference, which is huge in comparison to its small annual premium.

In conclusion, acknowledge that physical dangers surround us and that we're constantly at risk from without.

And, we're occasionally at risk from within: We still stick our fingers in the fan, despite the best efforts of our guardian angels to protect us. In fact, I suspect that you innately feel indestructible—which is not a knock against a young person. There's a monumental reason for this. God created you for eternity, and thus you sense the desire and expectation to live forever. A wise pastor of mine once pointed out that our souls and bodies weren't originally meant to be separated. Consequently, we fear—to our very depths—the concept of being torn asunder by death.

So, until we're raised on the last day, with glorified bodies like our Savior, insure yourself against what you can't afford to lose. And consider doing business with an independent insurance agent or financial planner, who should have your best interest in mind. If you're curious, here are explanations for the letters that follow the names of such professionals:

- CLU designates a Certified Life Underwriter.
- ChFC means that someone is a Chartered Financial Consultant.
- CFP signifies that he or she passed the comprehensive course to be called a Certified Financial Planner.

Chapter 8

THE FOUR WORK STRUCTURES
OF OUR ECONOMY

In no time at all, you'll be on the road to work or moving on to higher education—or maybe a combination of the two. In all cases, you're likely to gravitate toward people of like-mindedness. Wet concrete tends to separate its parts in the same way as it travels in a wheelbarrow over a bumpy path on the way to its destination. When you reach yours, you're expecting to find a comfort zone where you can ultimately break into a productive stride. But if you later don't like the place where you've plopped, you can get up and move. That, I believe, is one of your goals.

One of my goals is to help you be the cream on the top, as opposed to the rocks on the bottom. In this chapter, I describe our economy's four basic business structures, and comment on the advantages and pitfalls of each.

Our nation's federal, state, and local governments are, in reality, forms of business, and are referred to as America's **public sector**. Each of these three levels has a constitution to prevent its transformation into something it's not and a department of revenue to keep its checkbook full. Elsewhere are theocracies, parliamentary democracies, kingdoms, dictatorships, and communist and socialist countries. To stay out of the deep end, it's best to a leave a thorough examination of any and all forms of government to books on the political science shelf. Sorry, I can't help you establish a town or make you a ruler.

For the purposes of this chapter, I consolidate our public sector into one way to work. Combined with the three that follow, these are the chapter's four ways to work. (Actually, there are two more, but I'm going to skip the black market and underground activities.)

The sole proprietorship, the partnership, and the corporation are the business structures in our **private sector**. Each of the four has unique characteristics, in addition to its stated purpose and primary objective—which are two different animals.

Don't worry, there won't be a test afterward. In fact, completing this chapter won't show up on your transcript. It will, however, definitely make some college classes easier. Not only that, but you absolutely can't go around not knowing the basics of our economy and still expect to participate in its rewards.

The Public-Sector Businesses

America's governments—federal, state, and local—are "of the people, by the people, and for the people," if you'll allow me poetic license from Abraham Lincoln. Their shared purposes include providing the facilitation of self-governance; a legal system; an educational system; border defense; regulatory bodies for the public and private sectors; building and maintaining our infrastructure; and, among other things, the delivery of a variety of social services programs.

A shared objective of these governments is to make all the above happen efficiently, equitably, and economically—but not profitably, in the common sense of the word. That gives our governments and their agencies a pile of public-service work to do. Like magnets, these institutions attract people who enjoy running day-to-day operations—thereby creating careers in finance, utilities, defense, public safety, watchdog organizations, and administration, to name just a few. Those who join are public servants in the truest sense of the word, and my hat is off to them. Salaries and select total compensation packages can run parallel with those in the private sector, as the two compete for qualified personnel.

Through God's grace, some citizens aspire to work for justice and economic equality by running for legislative and political offices. Robert La Follette, the late Wisconsin governor and famed US senator of the 1920s, said it well: "Politics is economics in action." By definition, joining the public sector weaves you in with politics.

Expansion or contraction of either sector is influenced by which political party is in power. Conservatives on the right generally favor smaller, less regulated government. The further you move in that direction, the more you encounter unbridled capitalism and a survival-of-the-fittest mentality. Liberals on the left view things differently, and the further you go in that direction, the more you encounter meticulous regulation, which at its core is designed to thwart abuses of capitalism. Too much regulation, however, ties up an honest, budding entrepreneur in expensive red tape. And top socialist leaders on the extreme left believe they're smarter than the rest of the citizens, and dictate all the rules.

Extremes on either side can both lead to chaos. On the very far right, no one is in charge after a dictator is assassinated. On the very far left, everyone is in charge—which, again, means no one is in charge. Hopefully our left and right will keep us centered as the two viewpoints play tug-of-war.

Technically, our public sector is answerable to voters instead of shareholders, yet this is not true for everybody. Job security in the public sector is higher at the bottom than the top—especially when it comes to heads of institutionalized agencies (sometimes referred to as "deep government") and leaders of governmental worker unions. They all want to maintain the status quo.

Figure 8-1 shows a basic **corporate organizational structure.** Such a hierarchy leads to departmental accountability and an increased effectiveness of delivering products and services. It's common that a government will structure itself similarly, plugging in mayors and council members in place of CEOs and vice presidents. For example, figure 8-2 shows how the city of Champaign, IL has designed itself to accomplish these noble objectives.

Figure 8-1   Corporate organizational chart

In broad terms, our private and public sectors have admirably respected each other's boundaries. Our governments don't compete on supermarket shelves, and private enterprises don't offer alternatives to your city's water works.

As we head backstage on a guided tour of the sole proprietorship, the partnership, and the corporation, I might mention that all of them frequently describe themselves as a company—a group of people working toward a common purpose. The "busyness" you see on stage, for instance, is a dance company's attempt to convey the artist's message. Nonetheless, its business structure could be any one of the three. No matter how our private enterprises label themselves, their primary purpose may range from producing food, clothing, and shelter to providing

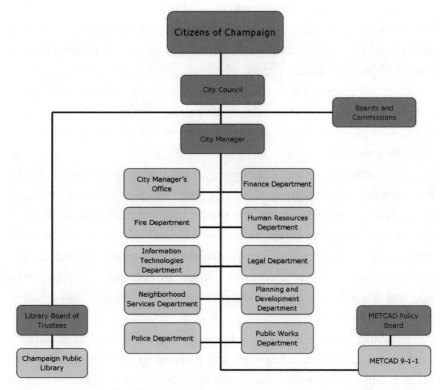

Figure 8-2   City of Champaign organizational structure (Courtesy of the City of Champaign, IL.)

human services, etc. With the exception of nonprofits, their sole objective is making money.

Some private-sector companies have been running profitably for quite a long time. The Shirley Plantation in Virginia bills itself as the oldest business in the States. Founded in Virginia in 1613, it has been owned and operated as a family operation since 1638. In searching the Internet for the world's oldest company, I found references to the Kongō Gumi Company in Japan. This construction firm traces its origins back to 578 AD, when it began building Buddhist temples. These examples of extended lifespan demonstrate that business ownership can be passed on, well after its founders have done the same.

A business can change structure along the way. For instance, beer-loving Fritz might start a microbrewery as a sole proprietorship and then sell it profitably to Anna and Naomi, who thus create a partnership. As success comes, the girls might change the arrangement into a corporation, and may ultimately put all their shares on the stock market. Meanwhile, back at the ranch, nothing changes for the employees. They just stay busy brewing suds according to the founder's recipe.

To be able to sell the microbrewery, Fritz had to first create an ongoing business. The reality is that, if going into business does nothing more than providing a living, the owner has nothing to fall back on at the end. An **ongoing business** is an operation with an established customer base; a product or service in demand; and, most importantly, the ability to run itself—regardless of changes in ownership. It has grown up, and has a life of its own, supporting various owners and creating countless jobs.

It would be nice if selling a business worked as well as drawing a card, reading, "Collect a big wad, and proceed to retirement!" Business brokers will tell you otherwise. Small businesses can be about as hard to sell as they are to grow. For one thing, potential buyers just don't have that much cash, and banks are reluctant to finance entire purchases. Sometimes a motivated owner will agree to a small down payment and sign a long-term **promissory note**. The slang term for this arrangement is "holding paper." Would you be up for trading your $750,000 business for an IOU that calls for payments over twenty-five years? What could go wrong, eh?

The question for older people then becomes, "What are some good strategies for getting my money out with minimal hassle and maximum profit?" That problem may not be relative to you today—and it may be too late for them to start thinking about the issues late in life—but you young entrepreneurs can benefit by knowing the characteristics of available business structures, and by choosing the one that's best suited for your anticipated life's work.

Shingle Example

On the day that owners hang out their shingle (like the sign shown here), they set measurable goals and develop actionable plans—all designed to create an income-generating and potentially marketable enterprise. Luckily, they seek talented people like you, who share their vision.

To add interest to our exploration of the private sector, let's follow the story of Francisco, a young man who joined the race and donned his thinking cap as soon as the green flag dropped.

The Sole Proprietorship

The **sole proprietorship** is the business model upon which the other two structures base themselves and has been around since the earliest days. Per the IRS, sole proprietorships are owned by only one person.

But, you may ask, what of the nonincorporated small businesses owned by married couples? Doesn't the IRS consider a mom-and-pop to be of one flesh? Don't they affirm their oneness by filing a joint 1040, which includes an **IRS Schedule C** for business expenses and a Form SE? Not exactly. Depending on the arrangement of husband and wife duties, the IRS may rule the business to be a **qualified joint venture**. Married folks can also form a partnership, if it works out best for them financially. Before you start a business, single or otherwise, consult with a suitably trained attorney.

Francisco learned how to rebuild lawnmower engines at a summer job. He liked the craft so well that he enrolled in trade school and began working out of a garage—not unlike Bill Gates, cofounder of Microsoft—with a sign that read, "Cisco's Small Engine and Machine Repair." He supplemented earnings by sharpening mower blades, working on outboard motors, and selling commonly needed parts. In winter, the kid concentrated on snowblowers, snowmobiles, and any small engine that powers a variety of machines. It wasn't long before he was starting to be known as the go-to guy in town.

Our hero understood that sustained growth is essential to any operation, and sought to expand his company by capturing commercial business and moving into new-equipment sales. To accomplish the former, Cisco hired a mechanically inclined part-timer and started his

A Nonfictional Entrepreneur

understudy on the time-consuming work. That enabled our entrepreneur to get out and knock on landscaping and construction company doors.

Expanding his inventory had to come next, so Francisco gathered his "books"—his financial records—and went to see his banker. A loan was approved by committee the following week, and Cisco placed a whopping order. The business plan worked, and the big boost in revenue allowed our protagonist to hire knowledgeable people in the service, parts, and sales departments—though this didn't happen overnight.

Importantly, he was able to retain his employees with a family-like atmosphere and better-than-average compensation. Francisco may have taken a cue from Henry Ford, who in 1914 nearly doubled his factory workers' wages to five dollars per day. Industrialists of the day thought he was wacko, and figured the move would bankrupt the automaker. Ford would prove his critics wrong. In just a few years, company profits soared. Some argued back that he raised wages so his employees could afford Model Ts. Regardless of his motivation (which Mr. Ford alone in heaven knows), it changed the dynamic in employer/employee relations. Both parties benefited.

Cisco hired a knowledgeable young lady named Lucia to assist him with important administrative aspects, knowing that his operation had to meet fair labor law, **OSHA (Occupational Safety and Health Administration)** requirements, and federal hiring practices—to name but a few. Within months, she was helping him pay bills, prepare payroll, and submit quarterly payroll and sales-tax reports. Within two years, Lucia was the office manager.

Francisco kept his books himself, at first—formal records comprised of ledgers and journals. In his **sales journal**, Cisco recorded daily revenue. In his **ledger**, he recorded his trucks; new equipment and parts inventory; machinery and tools; and, lastly, his office furniture. These items, along with other touchable objects that have a discernible life and purpose, are defined by accountants as a company's **tangible assets**. **Intangible assets** are those that you can't hold in your hand. An example is the value of an exclusive sales contract—like being the only one licensed to sell bottled water in the Gobi Desert. Another intangible is **goodwill**. Its main components are a loyal customer base, a good reputation, and, perhaps, a recognizable brand—including the company's logo. When you list a business for sale, you add a subjective dollar amount for intangible assets.

Francisco pulled data from his journals and ledgers to create two standard accounting documents called **financial statements**, or simply financials. They show the health of a business. The **profit and loss statement** (P&L) is nearly self-explanatory. Revenue for the measured period is listed in the top section, and same-period expenses are itemized in the lower section, and then totaled. **Net profit** is the amount by which total revenue exceeds total expenses. The **balance sheet** has a less descriptive name. In its top section, Cisco listed all tangible and intangible assets, along with corresponding dollar values. In its bottom section, he listed the expansion loan and other liabilities—such as accrued payroll, truck loan, and mortgage balance. Francisco's **owner's equity** is the mathematical difference between the two section totals.

His financials showed a sustained, healthy profit and a sizable business equity. Considering this data and his talented workforce, Francisco was confident that he had an ongoing business in the works. But the boss knew that he couldn't rest on his laurels. A rise in his income, and that of his employees, depended on further growth—driven, in part, by a second location.

Commercial State Bank said that it would surpass lending guidelines for such a loan, and suggested he consider **private equity financing**. Private equity firms fall within the **secondary lending market**, and aren't regulated as financial institutions are. As seen on reality TV, power players are willing to bring to market innovative products and services that banks won't touch. For instance, if the Wright brothers had approached Stuffy State Bank to help get their idea off the ground, it would likely have told Orville and Wilbur to go fly a kite.

Though he kept the advice under his cap, he studied the following business structure.

The Partnership

Francisco suspected he could help his business flourish by taking on a partner. The infusion of permanent capital avoids the need for loan payments, and the expertise of one or more like-minded people gives a concern more upside potential. On the downside, the move precipitates a **dilution of interest**. Cisco would then be sharing his profits and asset ownership.

As with a sole proprietorship, a partnership isn't subject to income tax *per se*. Instead, profits and losses **pass through** to the partners. Whatever that amount is, it goes on the person's individual 1040 tax return. Annual partner income (or loss) is listed on **IRS Form K-1**. He or she doesn't' receive the customary W-2, in this case. Any partnership employees, though, receive a W-2.

His first thought was that of his friend, Matthew, with skills and a plentiful net worth of his own. Should he bring on Matt as a co-owner, they would create a **general partnership** (GP). If a deal was struck, an attorney would need to draw up a partnership agreement and file a certified copy with the secretary of the state. (States regulate GPs.) Unless stated otherwise in the agreement, Matthew—as the new partner—would be liable for all existing partnership debt, and this new entrepreneur would now be obliged to contribute half the money to meet any shortage in future operational expenses. Because Francisco and Matt would own the business assets together and split annual profits, Matt could lose part or all of his potential investment if "Cisco's" goes belly-up.

Any business agreement should spell out duties and responsibilities, and should also address future scenarios, such as stipulating remedies for potential conflicts. Here's an important one: Just suppose that you're in partnership with a married individual, and that person dies prematurely. By law, that event immediately puts you in partnership with the deceased partner's wife or husband, as the case may be. If you wouldn't want the partnership to continue under those circumstances, then you and the original partner would have wanted to sign a **buy-sell agreement**, or some form of a **cross-purchase agreement** beforehand. Typically, examples say that in the event of a partner's death, the surviving partner gets first crack at buying out the interest of the deceased party. As a way to come up with the buyout money, partners can insure each other's lives with term life policies and designate each other as beneficiaries.

Scenarios can get complicated, and specific laws vary by state. As above, consult a competent attorney, and document the terms you and your partner agree to.

Rather than creating a GP, Francisco can bring on an investor looking for a financial return on a lump investment but who wants no involvement in running the show. That arrangement makes for a workable **limited partnership** (LP). Maybe Francisco will find Gloria? She's a busy, successful attorney who is willing to kick in 25 percent. Gloria might agree to the deal, after having her accountant review Cisco's books. Once again, a customized partnership agreement will be filed with the secretary of state.

However, here's how GPs and LPs differ the most: All that Gloria can lose if the enterprise fails is the amount she has invested. Her loss exposure to company debt and civil damages is "limited," even though her avenue for profit has no upper limit. After all, she has nothing to do with making operational decisions.

As general partners, Francisco and Matthew would have **unlimited personal liability** for business losses, and for civil and criminal judgments. The same holds true for owners of sole proprietorships. That's scary. If no resolution can be found for a loan default or a judgment, and the liquidation of your business assets doesn't satisfy the claim, courts can allow debtors to take your house, TV, and golf shoes. Business owners manage the risk of civil and criminal judgments through liability insurance with suitably set policy limits. They can further protect themselves from being personally wiped out by buying an umbrella liability policy.

The risk of unlimited personal financial loss for partners and sole proprietors can effectively be avoided if Francisco elects to go with the next business structure.

The Corporation

The noun "**corporation**" is a derivative of the Latin word *corpus*—or body—and serves as the underlying concept. Even your secretary of state, who grants its charter, treats it as if it's a person—well, at least a living body. Confused? Think of your student body. Doesn't it remain a cohesive organization, despite the parade of underclassmen in and graduates out? This so-called body has been deemed in court to be a legal entity with the same rights, privileges, and responsibilities that you have. Because it's an inanimate concept, it can't die. Therefore, the rascal can march on in perpetuity, while the members within it come and go.

Some states regulate rather strictly, and tax corporations quite heavily, while others tend to create an atmosphere conducive to business operation and expansion and lower their tax rate. The state of Delaware is one such jurisdiction, and some of the world's largest companies headquarter there for these reasons. When a corporate board of directors doesn't find what it wants at home, the members search offshore for lenient tax laws, etc.

If a corporation is an entity with rights and privileges, then it follows that it can own assets and real estate, and operate a business. Commercial, governmental, nonprofit, charitable, religious, and philanthropic organizations select the corporate structure for its effectiveness in meeting their varied objectives. The corporation is a hierarchical structure, with authority at the top and a chain of command that links together everyone below.

The Figure 8-1 organizational chart illustrates its purpose beautifully. A board of directors governs a corporation but, most often, the person with the most vested authority is the CEO. From there on down, you'll find any number of presidents and vice presidents—right down to the one in charge of picking up doughnuts. When municipalities choose the advantages of the corporate structure, titles such as commissioner, mayor, alderman, and various department heads replace corporate titles. Uncle Sam, for example, recognized how well-suited the corporation is to running a business, and settled on that for the Federal Deposit Insurance Corporation.

The Nonprofit Corporation

The first type of corporation to spotlight is the **nonprofit** (or not-for-profit). Does the name signify that it doesn't, or can't, make money? No, quite the opposite. In fact, it had better run profitably if it wants to stay in business.

Congress resolved that when a corporation specifically states in its charter that it exists to serve a segment of the population and those earnings are returned to that population, the IRS may deem that such earnings will not be subject to federal income tax, and will issue its 501(c) designation upon application approval. Not all charitable organizations meet the IRS qualifications for a tax-exempt status. Those that do are allowed to state so on donation receipts.

You don't have to look far to find a qualifying 501(c)(3) example. Your church is most probably one. Its primary corporate objective is that of leading souls to heaven. As noted in the tax chapter, this tax exemption permits churches to accept your offerings and donations without a tax consequence, and it allows you to use such as a tax-deductible expense.

All nonprofits must use generally accepted accounting practices (GAAP). You may have noticed in your pastor's annual report that the total of offerings, donations, and fall festival receipts were exactly the same as last fiscal year's church expenses.

Finally, a nonprofit (or any company) may decide that having an outside party audit its books is worth the added expense. A thorough auditor will find evidence of embezzling or spot irregularities that would cause the IRS to rescind the operation's tax-exempt status.

Francisco's objective is making money, so I'm sure he'll scratch this corporate variation.

The Publicly Held Corporation

Household names of **publicly held corporations** include Ford Motor, Apple, and Microsoft. Such a corporation must have four essential elements to qualify:

- **Transferable shares.** Cells are to a human body as shares are to the corporate body, though not nearly as many. Nonetheless, a company can have shares numbering into the tens of millions. They are transferred to other people by trading in their respective stock markets.
- **Indefinite life.** Like a school's student body, a corporation assumes an indefinite life as its shareholders trade their interests via the stock market exchanges.

- **Subject to taxation.** Corporate tax rates change, as corporate leaders lobby Congress for ways to reduce them. Results vary with political winds. Corporate dividends—which represent excess earnings—are targeted for tax, as well. This amounts to **double taxation.** And finally, not only are corporations subject to federal, state, and local taxes but, if they are multinational firms, they'll additionally pay foreign taxes and possibly franchise fees (taxes in disguise).

- **Limited shareholder liability.** Governments said that if a corporation was "born," as corporate attorneys successfully argued, and became an entity, it has to be held answerable to society for any harmful products, wrongful actions, unpaid debts, and problems caused by its errors. Incorporating protects shareholders who have no hand in the operation. Without some common-sense rules, defective products or actions could pose a big problem. For instance, poor Mike in Detroit Lakes, Minnesota, who holds ten shares of auto stock, could otherwise be held partially liable for death, personal injury, or property damage caused by a defective brake design at his Detroit, Michigan factory. Limited shareholder liability puts that scenario out of bounds.

If a corporation loses a civil lawsuit, the concept of limited liability doesn't preclude it from being held liable for damages. Money will flow out of corporate treasuries to meet judgments and fines. Furthermore, if it is proven that willful acts of corporate officers brought about public harm, then convicted executives can go to prison.

Corporations can go out of business as well. Just as the one-room schoolhouse disappeared because it became irrelevant, horse-drawn buggy manufacturers that didn't switch to car bodies closed up when automobiles appeared. Some American automakers nearly mismanaged themselves into oblivion by being unresponsive to market demands and failing to meet foreign competition.

Crooked business practices and immoral behavior are but two reasons that a secretary of state will pull the plug on any business structure deemed to be a threat to society. Late in 2017, the *Los Angeles Times* reported that such was the case with DaVinci Biosciences and its sister company. The California-based companies reached an expensive settlement over certain allegations. District Attorney Tony Rackauckas announced that "These companies will never be able to operate again in Orange County or the state of California" (see the link to the story at the end of this chapter).

Whoever's at the corporate helm makes a company a devil or an angel. An award-winning Canadian film by Mark Achbar, Jennifer Abbott, and Joel Bakan, titled *The Corporation*, examines boardroom objectives—both good and bad. In addition to being on the big screen, it has been shown in many high schools, and hope is that the work will influence business ethics, and aid in sustainability and environmental education. Perhaps you can convince your educator to see this hard-hitting analysis. (By the way, a sequel is planned.)

Theoretically, Francisco could join the ranks of people such as Facebook's Mark Zuckerberg by offering treasury stock to the general public. This is known as **going public**. This would inject a ton of permanent capital. The process would also be very expensive, considering the financing costs and attorney fees generated to satisfy federal and state filing and reporting requirements—not to mention associated printing and distribution costs.

Where would you start? Cisco did his homework and learned that he would have to bring his proposal to an investment-banking firm, maybe on Wall Street. That organization would front the money needed to hire the stockbrokers who would, in turn, market the new shares of, say, Cisco, Inc. This would be the company's **initial public offering**, or IPO, in the **primary sales market**. If an investor wants to trade them later, that would happen in the **secondary sales market**, understood to be the stock market. Francisco and his investment banker would design a sales plan that would leave our entrepreneur with enough shares to retain a controlling interest—assuming that the IPO is successful.

"It won't work," Cisco realized, after waking from his dream. "I face an issue more daunting than high costs and the risk of a blowout. My business isn't comprehensive enough in size or scope to bridge the chasm that divides me and institutional providers of goods and services. I guess it's back to the drawing board."

The Private Corporation

In discussing the matter with his CPA, Cisco discovered that he could quite easily and inexpensively convert his sole proprietorship into a **private corporation**. This variation is often a perfect fit for families or other closely knit group of people, who seek the safety and characteristics that a publicly held model affords. It isn't necessary to go into the all rules here, but know that Cisco and his key employees, as a group, would own and control every single share of stock. No closely held shares are ever for sale on Wall Street because of the company's private nature. Nevertheless, one can sell shares if one wants out of the business. But because private companies aren't subject to public financial disclosure, finding a buyer becomes more challenging.

Small, privately held companies comprise an enormous portion of our economy, but not all of them are little. Those of you in the southeastern US who shop for groceries at Publix are customers of what may be the largest employee-owned company in the world. And you'll find Johnson's Wax and its Ziploc containers on its shelves. These are products of S. C. Johnson, another huge, old, multinational private company. Lutheran High School and St. Catherine's in Racine, WI, are nearly neighbors with company headquarters.

The Subchapter S Corporation

Lastly, Francisco's advisor told him about the **subchapter S corporation**. It's a closely held company, as well. The corporation's handle comes from the portion of IRS law spelling out the rules and regulations that govern it. Among them, the IRS says that the number of shareholders can't exceed one hundred individuals—and they have to be American citizens. The subchapter S is a hybrid. It offers the liability-protection benefits of a corporation and the tax benefits of partnerships and sole proprietorships. All profits and losses pass directly to the stockholders at their respective tax rate, instead of corporate earnings being double-taxed. Owners receive an IRS Form K-1 at year-end, while employees receive a W-2. Considering Francisco now has fourteen key employees and workers at several locations, it's a most excellent choice for a larger group of unrelated business owners.

Cisco has been mentoring and compensating his employees well all along, and it has crossed his mind to establish an **ESOP**. The acronym sounds like Aesop, but has nothing to do with the Greek fable-teller. It stands for **Employee Stock Ownership Plan**, which is a vehicle that select employers use for cash-alternative compensation and to effect an eventual change in ownership. And it's a performance incentive, which will often attract even more good workers. Employees share responsibilities with owners, and everyone sees benefits down the road. Instead of receiving a full check, participants buy a little stock with the difference.

Joseph Pearce, a senior contributor at the *Imaginative Conservative*, told the story of Gellert Dornay, who gave away his mortgage-banking company, Axia, to his employees in 2016, using an ESOP; a URL at the end of this chapter leads you to the story. You can also search for Gellert Dornay and read more of his Catholic story. In the same essay, Mr. Pearce wrote about Ernest Bader—a Quaker, who transitioned owner-ship of his company to his employees, too. It's now called Scott Bader Commonwealth, which has turned into a very successful multinational chemical company.

ESOPs vary and are comprehensive in scope. They must comply with a federal-law package called ERISA, which may sound like the name of a girl you know. If one is ever rolled out by your employer, you'll get the details then.

Variations

You may have seen designations such as LLP and LLLP. An LLP is a limited liability partnership, and an LLLP is a limited liability limited partnership. These were created for unusual circumstances and specific purposes, and fall outside the scope of this book.

The Limited Liability Company (LLC)

The letters you want to pay attention to are **LLC**. They designate a **limited liability company**, which is a major business structure in the United States these days. Groups of physicians within a related field have formed LLCs to work together. The publisher of this book, which works with hundreds of authors, has done the same.

An LLC affords the pass-through tax advantages of the partnership, or sole proprietorship, and shelters the owners from liability like a corporation does—thus making it a hybrid entity. It requires less paperwork and reporting, and set-up costs are quite reasonable. If, one of these days, you want to start a business, speak with an attorney to see if an LLC would be a fit for your idea.

The Rest of the Story

All of the above have been created to protect providers and consumers of goods and services from wrecking each other through willful abuse.

As we close, I'll let you pick up where we leave Francisco. You might follow in his footsteps, or be equally comfortable as one of his managers or employees. As you develop, so will your opportunities.

Some people simply plateau—learning and development have ceased to be important virtues. Physics states that a body at rest tends to stay at rest. That's not the end of the world, I guess, if the kids are raised and people are well into retirement. It's a different story if the subjects are young and capable. Those who try to make careers out of entry-level jobs come to mind. These positions are reserved for you and your generation. They are training grounds, in two ways. First, you're taught the task at hand, and then you learn by observation how each job and department fit into the big picture—with knowledge coming faster at a small business.

Regardless of size, operations don't generate enough profit to turn minimum-wage jobs into something they're not. Occupants are expected to move up once they've gotten their feet wet in the income stream. This isn't simply a capitalist notion, nor is it a conservative political statement. From our Lord's parable in Matthew 25, we've come to understand that, even from those of us who have received little, God explicitly expects a return on the talent He invested in us. That's quantum. We do no eternal favors to needy but capable people by merely providing material support. We must teach a man to fish, and tell him why that's important—to both of us. That's true charity.

In reading the twelfth chapter of Paul's first epistle to the Corinthians, I can't help recognizing an analogy between the workings of our modern workplace and their church-at-large two millennia ago. A scriptural scholar may be able to tell us what prompted the saint to include this chapter, but it appears that some members may have been discussing inclusion and exclusion, and there could have been dialogue about who had the cooler spiritual gifts. Was it the one with the word of wisdom? Was it he with the word of knowledge—of working miracles— perhaps of prophecy?

Paul goes on to compare the mystical body to the human body and its parts—both seemingly important and unimportant, both shown and not shown, but all of which are essential and deserve respect. By the time he wraps up, Paul is telling us that as Christ's followers, we need to respect each other and get along. In the workplace, we too have different talents and various roles to play—seemingly important and unimportant, both behind the scenes and in the public eye—yet the work to be accomplished can only be achieved together.

We don't all need to be company presidents. The world needs talent across the employment spectrum. Even though advancement opportunities ahead are exciting to envision and work toward, we shouldn't forget that our Lord—as a carpenter—sanctified all states of life. In that light, getting to know yourself, finding your niche, and getting on with business will spell success differently for you than for others. The job/career-hoppers, who view the grass as greener on the other side of the fence, are those for whom it takes longer to figure this out. (I know it did for me.) In terms of forfeited retirement benefits and self-satisfaction, the cost for restlessness can be quite high.

Helpful Links

Oldest Companies

http://www.shirleyplantation.com

The film *The Corporation*

www.thecorporation.com

Joseph Pearce article

http://www.theimaginativeconservative.org/2017/06/turning-employees-business-owners-joseph-pearce.html

DaVinci Biosciences story

http://www.latimes.com/local/lanow/la-me-fetal-tissue-20171209-story.html

Chapter 9

STOCKS AND BONDS MADE SIMPLE

If you're joining the workforce directly after graduation, you'll quickly come face to face with **securities**. They comprise the heart of the long-term savings plan offered to new employees. And, as you'll learn in the next chapter, your participation will let you pick up free money off the table. If more schooling is ahead, or if you don't find a savings plan at work, you'll need to create a home-savings plan to keep pace with your friends who have the employer-sponsored plan—and maybe the individual one, too. By the end of this chapter, you'll have the confidence to make good stock and bond choices and won't have to depend on an HR clerk to teach you during the last few minutes of orientation.

I used to wonder why stocks and bonds are called "securities," since there certainly is no guarantee that owning such investments will leave you better off. It's more important to know that stocks and bonds are the elephants that carry the world's economy, and you don't want to be at the back of the line.

Each of these financial instruments has a straightforwardly defined set of rules, with very little of the fine print with which people should be rightly concerned elsewhere. They've been created with human integrity and personal honor in mind. Rapscallions who manipulate and distort these basic concepts are the ones who cause so much federal and state regulation.

I regret not educating myself on securities when I was younger. Despite media invitations as far back as I can remember, I ignored the print and TV attention dedicated to financial news and allowed the topic to remain not much more than white noise. Eventually, I got my feet wet as the **passive investor** who relegates stock and bond selections to professionals. Specifically, I bought into a mutual fund, which is a suitable investment vehicle for those who aren't active investors. I could have dived headfirst into securities by opening an individual brokerage account. That would have made me an **active investor**. I probably would have drowned, though, from lack of experience; having a poor understanding of the nature of securities; and trusting that financial advisors would place my best interest in front of theirs—which may have been silly of me to think so. The danger of going under is of little threat to you, as a minor, because you're legally precluded from being either type.

But time's nearly up. When you turn eighteen, the world expects you to be a competent passive investor, and it really cares less whether you've been suitably educated or not. By the end of this section, you'll have a working knowledge of stocks, bonds, and mutual funds, and will get a glimpse into the workings of an individual brokerage account.

We begin by looking at securities in general.

Securities Industry Regulation

The **Securities and Exchange Commission** (**SEC**)—consisting of five presidentially appointed commissioners—was created as part of the Securities Exchange Act of 1934, and, in its words today, is "designed to restore investor confidence in our capital markets by providing investors and the markets with more reliable information and clear rules of honest dealing." Accordingly, various divisions of this federal agency promulgate and enforce industry regulations, and the greater body provides an authoritative educational forum. Rules and regulations are applicable not only to brokerage firms, investment banks, and securities markets (such as the stock exchange on Wall Street), but to individual investors, as well. I encourage you to click on the tabs of the SEC website, where you can learn about a brokerage firm or investment advisor and can find in-depth studies of topics introduced in this guide. The tour will give you a broader exposure of the world with which you're soon to be engaged.

Brokerage houses are required to assess their customer's suitability to engage in trading as part of the effort to level the playing field. Brokers and **registered representatives** are obliged to "know their customers" through responses to a host of questions on the account application. SEC rules specify that to get into the game, active investors must have an established level of minimum net worth comprised of diversified assets and should possess some knowledge of the risks inherent in trading securities. It's a seller-buyer thing—just like a car dealer shouldn't have to teach you to drive.

Finally, the SEC, along with other federal authorities, can advise Congress and administrations about security-regulation changes if such seem warranted. And to avert a crisis, agency leaders can step in and take control if a market appears shaky, caused by any number of negative trading practices—thus underpinning the nation's financial integrity.

The **Financial Industry Regulatory Authority, Inc (FINRA)** is a self-regulatory organization (SRO) that exists to protect the trading public by policing the behavior of its member dealers. It is an independent corporation with regulatory oversight of more than 4,300 brokerage firms trading in equities, corporate bonds, securities futures, and options. The SEC approved its formation in 2007 to meet the major, contemporaneous recapitalization of the Nasdaq—a stock market that we'll cover with others. FINRA's predecessor was the National Association of Securities Dealers (NASD), which had been founded in 1939 to provide a similar role as it does today.

The testing and licensing of brokers and Registered Representatives are FINRA's obligations. Its respective department requires a high score on a comprehensive, rigorous exam (which can last up to six hours) before securities representatives can hold a Series 7 license, thereby allowing them to participate in a securities transaction. Top managers at investment firms must meet even stricter requirements, and are charged with ensuring that both licensees and non-licensed employees follow all rules of professionalism and ethical behavior. FINRA also provides educational seminars, and promotes efforts to keep the industry's image clean and polished. As with the guys and gals over at the SEC, men and women working at this organization wear the white hats.

Congress established the **Securities Investor Protection Corporation (SIPC)** in 1970, as another investor safeguard. Similar in purpose to the FDIC, this body indemnifies investors against fraudulent action and poor management by brokerage firms. I should stress that SIPC does not insure an investor's stocks and bonds against a loss in value, but stands ready to help if your investment firm goes belly-up or becomes financially troubled in a serious manner.

One trading risk not addressed by any regulatory body is that of falling prey to the "greater fool" theory. It contends, "There will always be some fool who will pay me more for this than I did!" For some in Europe during the early 1600s, living with the consequences of this supposition was bitterly painful. The experience had to do with tulips, of all things. While these flowers have always been prized for their beauty, the desire to own bulbs of rare varieties inordinately morphed from an appropriate appreciation into an obsession. (It's said that one poor soul had the stuffing beaten out of him after eating a prized one.) Those caught up in what started out as a craze began trading land, houses, and livestock to possess the most sought-after varieties, and "tulipmania" forced prices higher. More than six times an average worker's annual salary could be paid for one rare tulip bulb, and a record price was recorded for the Semper Augustus. It sold for about forty times the annual income of an average Dutch worker. When no one was willing to bid prices higher, the market plummeted. Those who were left lost their shirts, and the ripple effect of the burst bubble ravaged the European economy for decades. Presumably, some victims did themselves in—not unlike what happened following our 1929 stock market crash.

An anonymous Dutch artist of the 1600s immortalized the Semper Augustus in his or her painting shown here.

The next three sections of this chapter focus on aspects of the active investor and the securities markets, in general. As a savings-plan participant at work, you don't have to know this specific information because individual brokerage accounts aren't a part of a work savings plan. With that said, feel free to skip down to the section about stocks if you have no interest or want to save it for later. Nonetheless, you may find a trip down the pages enriching. I present the following for hungry readers, and to ensure that you get the full bang for your buck.

Semper Augustus (Source: Public Domain {PD-1923})

The Individual Brokerage Account

An **individual brokerage account** is the rudimentary form of securities ownership. Singles and families utilize it to increase their wealth by creating a **portfolio** comprised primarily of stocks, bonds, and mutual funds. The classic strategy for many (including professional brokers) is to accumulate and hold, and then adjust as necessary over time. Other players are the semiprofessionals, who spend most of their time at the computer. These **day traders** buy and sell online—often to the point of obsession. Knowledgeable ones can turn quite a profit. Less-skilled and poorly educated players amount to speculators, who hope to make a killing by buying low and selling high on particular stock issues. Both are born risk takers.

A **full-service brokerage house** can do everything for all traders. Their research department scours the globe for stocks and bonds and delivers those that meet the investor's criteria—including risk tolerance.

This comes with a price, of course. A single trade may cost you seventy-five dollars. But you can also trade online for much less, once you've established an account at a brokerage firm. A **discount brokerage house** may charge a fraction of full service, but historically haven't provided personal service, research, and advice. As investors become more educated and as competition between the two increases, they may look more similar than different.

Federal law requires all brokerage firms to document what you bought, when you bought it, and how much you paid. These factors determine the **cost basis** of each security. Furthermore, brokerage firms must report your profits, losses, and dividends to the IRS because Uncle Sam wants a slice of the pie. The percentage he takes is a function of time. A security held for more than a year is considered a **long-term position**, and when you sell it, even after more than fifty years, the IRS considers the difference between your cost basis and the trade price to be a **capital gain** or **loss**. If you have multiple long-term sales within a year, gains can be offset against losses. All net profit is taxed at the **capital gains rate**, which is a flat percentage set by Congress. During the last two centuries, that rate has fluctuated, depending on how DC policymakers felt. Historically, they have set it low because high rates discourage trading. If you buy and sell a security within a year or less, your position is considered a **short-term position**, and any profit is considered ordinary income, which is taxed at your individual rate.

Again, both full-service and discount brokers serve to execute your orders. For instance, you might want to buy a **round lot** (one hundred shares) of Ford. Fewer shares would be an **odd lot**. If you are willing to pay market price, your request will go in as a **market order**, which is good only for a day (**day order**). If, on the other hand, you aren't willing to pay more than a specific amount per share, you could place a **limit order**. Then, if Ford is trading at or below your top price, the order will get filled. If the market price is higher than your **limit price**, the order will simply expire at the end of the trading day. If you want to hang in there, in the hope of catching a lower price later, use a **good-till-canceled order**—or **GTC**. Don't concern yourself with memorizing the terminology—if and when you open an account, your broker will set you straight.

Upon a successful trade, your order will go to the appropriate exchange where the Ford-stock specialist will fill it. Your brokerage house will then post it to your account and send you a written **trade confirmation**. Keep that for your records.

The **three-day settlement rule** gives buyers time to come up with the money and allows the same to sellers in the event they hold certificates. Your broker is responsible for coordinating the event. In practice, the vast majority of securities are now registered within computerized accounts, and trades are accomplished nearly instantaneously.

Brokerage financing is available, as well. Firms are allowed by the Federal Reserve Board to lend qualified investors up to 50 percent of a stock's value, with interest. This is known as **buying on margin**. Details are spelled out under the board's regulation "T." **Leveraging your money** in this way can be profitable, but you must maintain a strictly enforced equity-to-loan ratio. If the margined security declines in value, the equity-to-loan ratio goes out of whack, which triggers a **margin call**. This system alarm requires that you add money to bring your account into compliance. If you don't have the money in your pocket, shares of stock will have to be sold at a loss to meet the call.

Here's another strategy to make money: You can sell a security that you don't own. The trade is known as a **short sale**, implying that you're short of what you're selling. What's the upside? Well, if you have reason to believe that the price of a stock you don't own is going to fall soon (you're **bearish**), you can place an order to sell and have the trade proceeds posted to your account. Then, because of the three-day settlement rule, you have both the time and money to buy the stock (that you'll need for delivery) at the lower price (assuming it falls) and pocket the difference. This is risky business to the uninitiated.

The acquisition process may seem strange at first, but it's really no different from moving elements across the equal sign in an algebraic expression. All that traders do here is change the conventional order of a sale, thus creating a derivational form of trading. This manipulation is called a financial "derivative"—or **derivative**, for short.

If you think the above is quirky, consider **option contracts**. These hypotheticals are imaginative to the third degree, and fully understanding option variations takes a great deal of studying. More importantly, making money in options demands even more experience.

In simplicity, option contracts allow you to trade equities at predetermined prices within predetermined periods. These federally regulated securities have an expiration date and a participation fee. Basic option contracts are named **puts** and **calls**, which trade on the Chicago Board Options Exchange (CBOE). The party who offers the security is the **option writer**, who owns that stock. The other is the buyer.

Let's first illustrate the **call option**. If you're **bullish** (believing that prices will rise) on a stock currently trading at $30, you could buy into a call option contract in a bid to make a profit on its anticipated upswing. In essence, you're saying to the writer, "I will pay you a fee up front for the option of buying your stock during the next sixty days at the $35 per-share price at which you've offered it." This dollar amount is the **strike price**. If the stock never moves to $35 before the option expires, all you will be out is the fee paid to the writer. This is what commonly happens. The majority of contracts expire harmlessly, and the option writer makes money. However, if the price moves to, perhaps, $40, you would "call" the option, and the writer is obliged to deliver the stock for $35, giving you a sweet $5 per-share profit.

On the other hand, if you're bearish on a stock, you could get into its **put option contract** in an attempt to score a profit on its falling share price. How? The contract allows you to sell that particular stock during a predetermined period for a predetermined strike price, and the other party is required to take it off your hands before you take a bath in it.

We've looked only at option basics. The sophistication level and risk tolerance required to trade options and their variations are quite high.

For example, you can initiate an option on an equity you don't even own—putting you in a **naked position**. You're vulnerable, and if things go wrong, your potential dollar risk is unlimited. The options section in the Series 7 securities exam gives test takers a migraine and dry mouth. Undaunted, some students of the art become experts at combining put and call options into formulas for protecting not only a singular stock position, but even an entire portfolio of securities. Traders hedge their losses with these "insurance" strategies by doing so. With that perspective, you may now have a rough idea of what a **hedge fund** is.

It may seem that derivatives amount to little more than legalized gambling. One junior asked, "Who makes up this stuff?" I told him that answer lies in the Golden Rule of economics: "Those with the gold make the rules."

The Stock Markets

Technological advances have reduced the employment level at brokerage houses, but not all jobs have been lost. Live brokers, traders, and specialists are still working to accomplish your trade on "the floor" of actual buildings. These structures house **stock exchanges**. Arguably, the most famous one is the New York Stock Exchange (NYSE) on Wall Street (nicknamed the Big Board). There and elsewhere, big brokerage houses own expensive **exchange seats** that allow them to conduct business on-site. Trading happens in Philadelphia, Chicago, and in more than a hundred exchanges worldwide, with representation on every continent except Antarctica. More than fifty countries, with their own exchanges, together comprise the elaborate "stock market."

Huge electronic exchange boards display trading activity with an alphabetic-symbol combination, rather than with a company name. For instance, Tiffany & Company's trading symbol is TIF. More precisely, that's its **ticker symbol**, which is reminiscent of the days when real-time trading was documented by a machine that punched out these symbols on a narrow roll of paper. This ticker-tape waste piled up, and, one day, some smart aleck in New York threw it out a window during a parade. With twenty-six English letters, there can be only that number of stocks with a single-letter symbol, and those few are cherished like great domain addresses. Ford Motor Company, for example, is known simply by capital F, and AT&T is recognized by T. A ticker symbol is handy for accessing current and historical trading data, as well as applicable news and opinions. Simply input it into the search box of a financial news website.

A portion of equities trade on the **National Association of Securities Dealers Automated Quotation** system (**Nasdaq**)—in Philadelphia, which is the oldest stock exchange in the US. This computerized trading extravaganza handles millions of trades per day. Here is where you find such tech stocks as Microsoft (MSFT), Intel (INTC), and Apple (AAPL). Again, a visit to the Nasdaq website will bring opportunities for industry discovery—perhaps even a career.

You don't have to be wealthy to acquire a fair number of shares in any one company. Offerings can be available at just a few dollars or cents. These are the **penny stocks**, and you can buy a round lot or less on the Nasdaq. Walmart began its meteoric rise as a penny stock. A great number of penny stocks don't trade on mainline exchanges, but are said to trade **over-the-counter**, and are available through brokerage firms and market makers who specialize in them.

Very little research is available on this class of stock, so it is difficult to evaluate a good deal. You can find some information about a company and its share's price and trading activity on the **Over-the-Counter Bulletin Board**, or **OTCBB**. If you would like to gain knowledge about the universe of penny stocks, type "information about penny stocks" into a search bar, and go from there.

Occasionally, investors visit chat rooms in a search for "hot" deals, but may, instead, encounter fraudsters. Here's one scheme: A sly character might own a penny stock and intentionally hype it up with quite convincing baloney. When unwary buyers take the bait, and start snapping up shares, its price rises. When the con man thinks the time is right, he sells out for a handsome profit. Despite the low prices, this minor league can be a volatile arena, and you shouldn't view it as a place to buy and sell as a game, yet it can be a place to learn.

Stock Exchange Indexes

A **stock exchange index** is a useful tool to gauge how a trading day is trending. The US has a number of indexes but, by far, the **Dow Jones industrial average** (DJIA) is the most famous. Charles Dow and Edward Jones developed this stock-direction indicator in the spring of 1896. Their comprehensive formula produces a number that is watched constantly worldwide. When the Dow is up, more stocks within it are trading higher in value than lower. The index, which is comprised of only thirty large publicly owned US companies, started out at well below 100—just look at where the Dow sits today! Listed companies come and go, as their influence in the economy builds or wanes.

Standard & Poor's—a provider of investment research and credit ratings—has a closely watched index, too. It has a different equity makeup and is called the **S&P 500**. Not to be left in the dark, foreign exchanges have their own indexes for guidance. The Japanese have the Nikkei; the Germans have their DAX; the French have the CAC-40; the FTSE-100 (the footsie 100) is in London; and the Hang Seng Index (HSI) lights the way in Hong Kong. And the EAFE offers a clue as to what is happening in Europe, Australia, and the Far East when trading is suspended elsewhere for the night.

Market and Stock Evaluation

The market is an irrational being, to say the least. Trying to forecast its movement or to understand its gyrations even in hindsight is challenging. A field of study has been built around this quest, and two schools of thought in economics have emerged. One takes a technical approach to predicting the direction of securities and markets, and the other holds a fundamental view of what's likely to transpire. **Technical analysts** study stock-price history, among other aspects, to predict its future movement. Important factors to them are price behavior, market cycles, trends, indexes, moving averages, and volume, to name but a few. The chart is to a technical analyst as a telescope is to an astronomer. **Fundamental analysts** examine the company's financial statements, world events, industry forecasts, and other factual data, including weather. They consider both quantitative and qualitative data and attempt to evaluate the mood of the market, consumer confidence, environmental impacts, and much more before making their buy or sell recommendations.

A number of stock-valuation methods are available to help stock pickers. In general, the methods fall into one of two categories—either an absolute or a relative-valuation model. All that I'll say here is that absolute models look at the fundamentals of a company's finances, and relative-valuation methods look at how a security stacks up against comparable ones, after being run through various cash-flow analyses.

I'll briefly illustrate one calculation that you hear a lot about but is of limited use. It's the **price/earnings ratio**, or **P/E**. You arrive at a stock's P/E by dividing its current price by its annual earnings—assuming that it pays dividends. For instance, if a stock is at $30 and its per-share earnings are $3, then dividing earnings into price yields an answer of ten. This quotient is called the **price multiple**, or multiple, for short. Typically, if the number is high within a range, it's rated attractive. In this case, the stock is generating a 10 percent rate of return. The multiple also indicates that it will take ten years for its earnings to recoup your investment.

Some of you will enjoy learning more about securities analysis, but none of you will be at risk right now if you don't. I've merely sketched equities valuation as its introduction. For now, your precious time is better spent focused on being your life's architect than on learning valuation science. In the end, investors often make selections based on some combination of stock-valuation study, intuitive sense, and emotion.

Again, there are two valid ways of being an investor. One is building a customized portfolio of securities by being an active trader, and the other is investing passively in mutual funds within or outside of an employer-sponsored savings plan. Both ways forward can be financially rewarding.

Stocks

Welcome back, if you sat that last section out. As mentioned, your first equity position is quite likely to be your participation in a work savings plan. Within it are mutual funds, and within mutual funds are a finite number of shares of stocks of a multitude of companies. When you select a stock-based mutual fund, you really and truly become part owner in those companies. We're here to learn about the characteristics of what you will own.

Stock is classified as either common or preferred. **Common stock** comprises the majority of a company's capitalization, and the trading market sets its price. Investors who buy **preferred stock** enjoy "preferential" treatment by getting first crack at the company's excess revenue—better known as dividends. The number of preferred shares issued is demonstrably lower, and price is understandably higher.

With an individual brokerage account, you can opt to receive a **stock certificate** upon purchase of either class, despite the fact that you will be formally registered as a shareholder. A certificate isn't needed. Long ago, they were popular with investors who casually bought and sold on corners, as opposed to the frenetic trading of today. I've reproduced a canceled B&O railroad certificate (yes, as in Monopoly) in figure 9-1. This original parchment-like document was issued in 1914. If you want to see a contemporary one, search on, say, "Apple stock certificate" and click on images.

As with similar negotiable instruments, its embellishments and signatures discourage fraud and counterfeiting. The disadvantage of holding a certificate is that it must be owner-endorsed and sent to the brokerage house to complete a trade, much as a car's title must be negotiated upon sale. Because mail delivery was slower in days of yore, that reality led to the three-day settlement rule.

Figure 9-1   Canceled B&O Railroad Certificate

Quarterly dividend news is important to shareholders and traders. The "street" (investors outside of an exchange) closely follows the forecast profitability of **listed companies** (exchange-traded) and becomes optimistic or pessimistic based on the board of directors' public announcement regarding company earnings, as well as the amount and timing of per-share dividends. Companies that regularly pay dividends are **income stocks**, which your grandparents favor. Alternatively, companies may issue fractional shares in lieu of cash, which may be right for you. By opting for a **dividend reinvestment plan**, or **DRIP**, you can make full-share purchases when you accumulate enough fractional shares. As a bonus, you won't have to pay a brokerage fee to do so.

Some organizations plow profits back into research and development, plant and equipment acquisitions, and marketing, etc. These are the market's **growth stocks**, which don't normally pay dividends. You assume higher risk by owning them, but they increase your potential for gain as a tradeoff. Search on the term "top growth stocks" to see examples.

Bonds

Near the end of Disney's animated feature film *Peter Pan*, Wendy warns Peter that Captain Hook is trying to trick him, after declaring that he'd fight Hook with one hand behind his back. Peter was about to do just that and refuses her caution with the reply, "No! I gave my word!" Oh, ancient sweet virtue, so universally admired and respected—central even to the boy who wouldn't grow up! We thank God for instilling this inclination to behave honorably—leading to respect and trust. Just as one's word is one's bond, a bond issuer gives its word that the debt will be repaid, along with quarterly interest payments. With this trust, we wake with optimism, and invest confidently. In the absence of trust, families could have remained small, isolated, protectionist units, thus schools, manufacturing plants, and airports couldn't have been financed.

Bonds trades occur between issuers and buyers in the **primary market**, and between individuals in the **secondary market**, both of which are done through securities exchanges. The earliest issuances didn't have registered owners and the government wasn't included. An old unregistered bond was called a **bearer bond**—implying that whoever possessed it was the owner. Each bond came with attached coupons stating the interest rate to be paid. The appendages were to be "clipped" quarterly and mailed to receive the earnings. (Scope out the one in Figure 9-2, which still has some attached.) Ergo, a bond's interest rate is referred to as its **coupon rate**. Bonds yield interest—not dividends. Stocks pay dividends.

It's possible that a few valid bearer bond certificates are still floating around, but because of their downside characteristics, issuing this type of debt instrument has gone the way of the dinosaur. One problem with these unregistered (hence, untraceable) securities is that if they're lost or stolen, their coupons can be clipped by someone else and the certificate can be surrendered for the principal amount by whoever possesses it. Another issue is that the IRS was in the dark on who to tax on earnings or profits upon disposition. Today, the bond issuer's **trustee bank** registers these debt instruments in your name and reports your earning to the IRS.

True to an economy split into private and public sectors, movers and shakers have created the corporate bond and a variety of government bonds.

Figure 9-2   Coupon Bond

Corporate Bonds

A successful **corporate bond offering** enables a company to borrow money from the general public for a long period of time. Brokerage houses market these debt instruments in $1,000 denominations, and then funnel the proceeds to the issuer through that trustee bank.

Here's a short hypothetical that illustrates the process and highlights bond characteristics: If, one day, Ford wanted to build a new truck plant, its board of directors would have evaluated financing options. Issuing more treasury stock isn't the most palatable option because doing so dilutes shareholder interest. (Think a thousand business partners, instead of four.) Would Ford borrow from a bank? Not likely. Bank loans are short-term obligations with high payments, which begin right away. Accordingly, that would devour working capital until the proposed plant was rolling out shiny new E-150s. Its best choice, the board may have determined, was to "float a bond," and turned that responsibility over to Ford's financing arm, Ford International Capital Corporation. That crew would have then placed a huge ad in *The Wall Street Journal*, advertising the new investment opportunity.

Figure 9-3 is a reproduction of a canceled bond certificate issued by Ford in 1968. You can buy a variety of originals like this on eBay and wallpaper your bedroom. As with the artful stock certificate, it's embellished with beautiful engravings and features an array of fonts and type sizes—all designed to proudly present the company's heritage and to instill investor confidence. I don't know if Ford wanted to build a plant with this one, but it's not important for our purpose.

Near the top appears the designation, "5% Convertible Guaranteed Debenture Due 1983." A **debenture** is a bond that doesn't offer any collateral. To make things official, the chairman of the board and an officer of the trustee bank sign at the bottom.

High on an investor's wish list is the bond's **yield**. Here, Ford promises 5 percent on this fifteen-year example. Success would give the

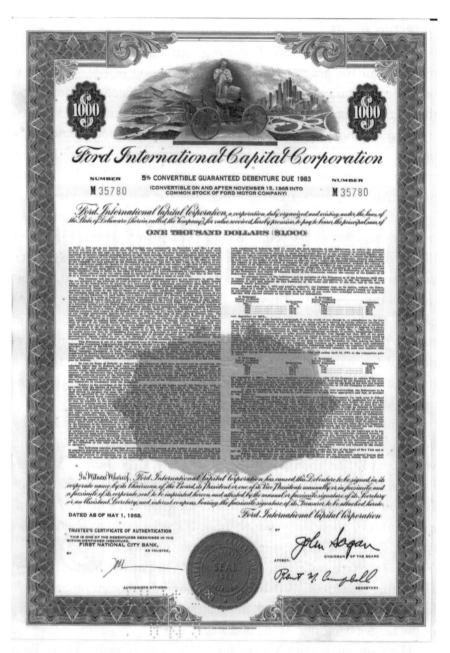

Figure 9-3   Ford Bond

automaker the time and money to build a plant, and would set aside enough of its revenue to repay bondholders by 1983.

Investors might have received their money early, under the right circumstances. One term specified is that Ford's board of directors reserved the right to retire the bonds ahead of time and subsequently cash out the investors as early as 1973. This feature makes it a **callable bond**. This **bond redemption provision** is typical. It's a refinancing avenue if future interest rates take a downward swing. To illustrate, if prevailing interest rates dropped to 2 percent in, maybe, 1972, Ford would likely call back this 5 percent debenture and issue a lower one. There's a table in the body that runs from 1973 through 1980, which guarantees that Ford will pay bondholders 100 percent or more of the bond's $1,000 face value in the case of a call. As we'll see later, bonds can trade for amounts lower or higher than face value. Coughing up a premium was the price Ford was willing to pay for gaining flexibility.

The certificate states that this is a **convertible debenture**. In our case, bondholders would have been able to surrender it for shares of common stock. Reading the bond would have told the investor when that would be a good deal: Terms specify that Ford would exchange the $1,000 bond for 14.49 shares. The quotient of dividing $1,000 by 14.49 is $69.13, which makes the bond equivalent to the number of shares at that value. If Ford's stock rose appreciably above that and was expected to continue appreciating, it would make sense to convert the bond into the more valuable shares.

If an investor wanted out before the bond matured, he or she could have traded it through a brokerage house. The biggest factor influencing the sales price is the prevailing interest rate for comparable investments. There's an inverse relationship between the two. When interest rates rise on investments like savings accounts, bond prices fall. And the opposite is true. To explain this phenomenon, let's say that you want to sell your 5 percent Ford bond and that interest rates on safe investments rise to, perhaps, 7 percent. Holding the bond would leave you with a dog (with apologies to Fido owners). Consequently, the bond will trade at a discount if you want to unload it. Let's guess that you might net only $900 on your $1,000 investment. On the other hand, if prevailing rates fall well below 5 percent, buyers will snap up your bond at a premium, and you might realize $1,100 or more on a trade.

Some measure of safety is important to even the riskiest of investors, because a percentage of these debt instruments default. To help investors measure that risk, bonds are examined for quality and ultimately rated. Standard & Poor's and Moody's are leaders in the rating industry, but neither can guarantee safety. Bonds rated AAA and BBB are considered **investment grade** (the highest quality), while those receiving a rating of BB or lower are lovingly referred to as **junk bonds**. But don't judge a book by its cover. Despite the fact that junk bonds are often offered by young, undercapitalized companies, their high yield commands attention, and can serve as a component of a well-diversified portfolio. And remember, a downswing in interest rates propels *all* bond values higher—causing them to trade at a premium.

A bond that sells at a discount right out of the box is called a **zero-coupon bond**. For instance, you may have to pay only $750 for a $1,000 bond that matures in ten years. The longer the term, the steeper the discount. The bond issuer doesn't make quarterly payments on a zero (also known as a **deep-discount bond**), thus allowing the issuer to use cost-free money for a long time. A buyer benefits because he or she can get into a security for less money. These rascals work well for younger investors, but not for retirees looking forward to quarterly checks.

Your return on a zero is its annual increase in value, or **accretion**. You can determine the bond's value by referring to a table, which specifies its annual appreciation. Perhaps three years after purchase at $750, it may be worth $832.54. Historically, annual bond accretion has been taxed, even though you don't receive a check—Uncle Sam doesn't want to wait until the end to get a share of the profits.

Zeros aren't the corporate bread and butter, but you will find examples by the billions gushing out of Washington, DC. The most prominent is the EE Savings Bond.

Government Bonds

Municipal Bonds

The **municipal bond** is a most popular debt instrument issued by a variety of public-sector authorities. States, counties, cities, school districts, and airports, for example, use these IOUs as means to fund projects like highways, schools, and runways. A "muni's" important characteristic is that its yield is generally exempt from federal, state, and local taxes. (Check with your tax consultant before buying. Laws can change nearly overnight, it seems.) This enviable tax-exempt status, coupled with a municipal's perceived safety, allows local government leaders to offer low interest rates as they compete in the marketplace with corporate bonds and those of Uncle Sam—which come next.

Munis can yield higher effective returns than a taxable bond at a higher rate. A **taxable equivalent calculation** shows the spread. The formula is the division of the municipal's yield by one minus your tax bracket. In the example below, I'm assuming a 35 percent tax bracket and using a 4 percent municipal. The math indicates, in this case, the municipal has the equivalent yield of a 6.15 percent corporate bond. Municipals become more advantageous as your tax bracket increases.

$$.0615 = \frac{.04}{(1-.35)}$$

Munis are not glamourous and exciting investments. So, to help catch an investor's eye, an issuer—such as a municipality—will choose to have its offering insured against default. This "lipstick" makes it more attractive, especially to a conservative investor. An insured AAA muni, for example, is about as safe as you can get. However, the insurance cost decreases the bond's yield slightly.

A municipal bond that's to be repaid with income or property tax is classified as a population's **general obligation bond**. One that's issued to build income-generating improvements—such as a toll road—is a **revenue bond**. And because mayors can't afford to simply write a check, an **assessment bond** might be utilized by a city to put sewer, water, and sidewalks into a new part of town, or to upgrade an old neighborhood.

A major source of an assessment bond's retirement is higher property taxes. Figure 9-2 above featured a street improvement bond issued by the city of Los Angeles in 1927; its face value was $196.52, and boasted a rate of 7 percent.

Proposed city and school-board bond issues draw attention and debate at public meetings. Some projects are controversial. The voices of well-educated citizens can bear influence on how a municipality expands. Overall spending has to be watched, so that the city's credit rating doesn't suffer. If a municipality defaults on a bond, it can cripple services and unduly burden taxpayers. Sadly, poorly managed American counties and cities have gone bankrupt. You can search their stories on the Web. But one day soon, you'll be both a taxpayer and voter.

US Government Bonds

The US Department of the Treasury offers a diversified assortment of bonds, classified as short, medium, and long-term. Worldwide, investors snap them up because Uncle Sam's obligations are considered the safest—considering the nation's status and the fact that the United States has never been in default. American debt ranks at the top of the investment grade bond chart. Here is a listing of offerings:

- **Treasury bills** are short-term obligations, with terms that run from a few days to a year. Commonly called T-bills, they're sold in $1,000 increments, but you pay less than that because they're of the zero-coupon type.

- **Treasury notes** feature a fixed rate of return and pay interest every six months, with terms of two, five, and ten years. Denominations range from less than $100 to $10,000.

- **Treasury bonds** are of the fixed rate and pay interest every six months, with terms of up to thirty years. That one is called the **long bond**. Denominations range from under $100 to $10,000.
- **Savings bonds** come in a range of choices. Denominations range from $50 to $10,000. They, too, are zero coupons. Under the **Education Bond Program**, savings-bond earnings may be free from federal taxes when used for higher education. Until recently, Uncle Sam issued savings bonds in hard copy, but that's no longer the case. Your proof of ownership exists in digital form, within the account you set up with the Treasury Department.

You can purchase all US Government bonds through a financial securities firm, a participating bank, or by going directly to the Treasury website. (Its link is at chapter's end.)

Income from federal Treasury bills, notes, and bonds, or income from a federal agency obligation is taxable for federal purposes but may be tax-exempt for state and local purposes. Check with your tax consultant.

Mutual Funds

As above, those of you joining the workplace will be eligible to own shares in one or more mutual fund choices in the very near future. So, let's take a look.

A **mutual fund** is a prepackaged, professionally managed selection of, predominantly, stocks and bonds. This investment vehicle became popular after the Depression because the rules under which it was created leave an investor less vulnerable to the inherent risks of trading. For example, a mutual fund cannot invest more than 10 percent of its total value in any one security and must buy at least ten different ones. This is known as **diversification**.

When you buy in, the mutual fund creator must give you a **pro-spectus**. This pamphlet presents important information, which include the fund's investment objectives, its strategies for achieving those goals, the principal risks of investing in the fund, all fees and expenses, and how well it has performed in the past. The investment objective might be investing in growth stocks, or government bonds, or perhaps it buys stock in companies that mine precious metals, like gold and silver. A mutual fund's colorful **annual report** is more fun to read. It introduces you to the fund manager and shows returns for the previous year. Graphs also illustrate what a hypothetical $10,000 investment is currently worth if made five and ten years ago. But don't infer that future performance will be indicative of past results. Lastly, annual report pages list the stocks and bonds that the fund bought—some of which you'll readily recognize.

Financial services companies assemble and market mutual funds, and the vast majority are termed **open-end funds**, implying that you can still buy in. The relatively small number of **closed-end funds**, however, are no longer available to new investors. There are also a growing number of **exchange-traded funds**, or **ETFs**. Owning these sophisticated securities requires a brokerage account.

The minimum investment for passive investors to open a common mutual fund account varies by company. Costs may range from $500 up to $3,000, but companies make exceptions for contributions to tax-qualified savings plans. A few will even let you buy in on the installment basis, with a bank authorization. Some recognizable mutual fund names are Janus, Fidelity, Putnam, Vanguard, and Oppenheimer, to name but a few.

Mutual fund shares are offered at its **public offering price**, or **POP**, and you'll pay a **sales charge** to join, in most cases. This fee helps offset broker sales commissions. When you sell shares, you receive their **net asset value**, or **NAV**. You earn a profit when the NAV rises above the sales charge plus the initial POP. A mutual fund's NAV is a distillation of all the stock, bond, and cash-equivalent values inside the fund, which is then divided by the number of outstanding shares at the end of the trading day. NAVs are found online by ticker symbol or by company name in the financial section of newspapers, like *The Wall Street Journal.* You can calculate the dollar value of your investment by multiplying the NAV times the number of shares you own. There's another fee involved besides the sales charge. Mutual fund companies are allowed to charge what's known as an annual 12b-1 fee. It can run from as little as a quarter to 1 percent of NAV.

Mutual fund companies must report your annual share of taxable capital gains and dividends and sends you a 1099 DIV for your tax return. You'll receive one even if you haven't sold any shares.

Respectively, mutual funds are known by three categories:

- **Front-load funds**. Front load fund companies carry class "A" shares, which subtract their advertised sales charge from the value of your initial investment. This cost can range from 3.75 to 5.75 percent and can be as high as 8.5 percent if it doesn't assess a 12b-1 fee. Search "best front-load mutual funds" to lead you lots of places.

- **Rear-load funds**. Rear load funds, also known as class "B" shares, assess a contingent deferred sales charge when you sell all or some of your shares. The idea is that all of your money goes to work right away earning returns. It may have to because rear-load fund expenses are typically higher.

- **No-load funds**. No-load funds advertise free admission, which is attractive. They are so because you usually purchase them directly from the mutual fund company, instead of through a financial advisor. As with discount brokerage houses, you don't get personal service or advice here.

There's more to read online. You can search "learning about mutual funds" to bring up a wide array of choices. Historically, Morningstar, Inc has been one of the best over the years. The information used to be free, and its website looked a lot different. Nonetheless, they may still have a 14-day free trial offer. It's an excellent place to learn about any mutual fund or investing in general. I invite you to poke around there to find news, research, forums, and more gadgets for your toolbox.

One mutual fund sector is dedicated to **socially responsible investing**, which may be of interest if you're reluctant to invest in companies that don't match your moral convictions. Some SRI funds (and individual stocks) invest in companies that protect the environment, respect workers' rights and dignity, and produce safe products. Others specifically avoid buying stock of companies engaged in vice and immorality. And you may be surprised at how well some of these funds have performed. A great place to learn more is the Forum for Sustainable and Responsible Investment.

As this philosophy gained traction in the minds of investors—both individual and corporate—it developed. Now we go by **Environmental**, **Social**, **and Governance** (**ESG**) criteria as standards to measure how a company's activity impacts mother nature and humankind, and how well it treats its employees. Check out the link to learn more. It might fit you some day. For now, you serve yourself best by establishing a cash reserve and formulating a budget—which we'll get to shortly.

With what we've covered you're now prepared for the very important next chapter, which almost certainly will be of use in your workplace.

Helpful Links

Securities and Exchange Commission (SEC)

https://www.sec.gov

Financial Industry Regulatory Authority (FINRA)

http://www.finra.org

Securities Investor Protection Corporation

https://www.sipc.org

New York Stock Exchange (NYSE)
https://www.nyse.com/index

National Association of Securities Dealers Automated Quotation system (Nasdaq)
https://www.nasdaq.com

Over the Counter Bulletin Board (OTCBB)
http://www.finra.org/industry/otcbb/otc-bulletin-board-otcbb

Learn about Investing at Morningstar
http://www.morningstar.com

Forum for Sustainable and Responsible Investment
https://www.ussif.org

Education Bond Program
https://www.treasurydirect.gov/indiv/planning/plan_education.htm

Buy Bonds from the Treasury Department
https://www.treasurydirect.gov/tdhome.htm

Chapter 10

SAVINGS PLANS AT WORK AND HOME

"Get signed up," the HR manager urged on orientation day. "This savings plan is part of your earnings, and if you don't enroll during an eligibility period, that part of your budgeted pay gets split among employees who've already taken the plunge."

"What? Why don't you just include it on my check?"

"Frankly, lawmakers think you'll just blow that money."

"Well, frankly, that's just none of their business!"

"Frankly, I can't necessarily say you're wrong. But despite how we feel, sometimes things are done for the common good."

The issue is that long ago, Americans didn't have a mandatory, uniform method for creating a reserve to draw from when their bodies fell behind in making repairs, nor did they have an optional, standardized savings plan at work. The only leg they had to stand on late in life was what they hadn't spent. Help came in the form of the **three-legged stool**. Social Security benefits constitute one support; savings plans at work are designed as another; and the third upright you'll need to build yourself. By the time we've studied all three components, you'll be qualified enough to draw up a blueprint for your own sturdy perch. As we go, I promise not to harp on retirement—in fact, I hesitate using the r-word in front of you. You see that day coming at a glacial pace—but in the words of a t-shirt I read, "I thought getting old would take longer."

Social Security Benefits

In surveying the landscape following the Great Depression, President Franklin Roosevelt didn't like what he saw. In 1935, plans were set into motion to help the suffering population. In a strike against widespread, crippling poverty, President Roosevelt and Congress mandated that employers withhold and send to a new federal agency 2 percent of all workers' earnings and save it for them. These wage deductions are known as **FICA**, which is an acronym for the "Federal Insurance Contributions Act." Gradually, withholdings increased to just over 7 percent. Furthermore, it was required that employers were to match the mandated amount and to submit the combined deposits quarterly. This new body assigned to each worker a nine-digit account number, which numerically worked its way from the eastern seaboard to the country's western boundary. It was dubbed the Social Security number. The intention was to prudently invest these contributions and return the money to account holders in their sixties via annuity payments—making Social Security the nation's first forced savings account. A nominal burial amount was included, as well.

Succeeding administrations established the Old-Age and Survivors Insurance Trust Fund (OASI) as the rich uncle who stabilizes the program. Later, others added the Social Security Disability program and underpinned it with the Disability Insurance Trust Fund (DI). Through a combination of factors and trends, including extending benefits to people who haven't paid into the system, Social Security benefits are projected to decrease in the coming years. According to the Actuarial Status of the Social Security Trust Funds summary released by the Social Security Board of Trustees in June 2018, the combined trust fund-reserves are drawing down, and if no changes are made to the program, they'll be depleted in 2034. At that time, benefits will be supported solely by contributions, and it will then pay only 79 percent of program cost.

Even with the possibility of sweeping reform legislation, fewer people qualifying for Social Security Disability, and a shift toward national austerity, the health of the Social Security system shouldn't be counted on to stabilize your perch. Again, it really wasn't intended to.

Savings Plans at Work

Various programs that reward longtime workers have been part of the equation for centuries—but not for everybody. Not spreading the wealth very well has been a criticism of capitalism. In 1974, Congress enacted the Employee Retirement Income Security Act (ERISA) to induce more employers to establish equitable plans for both themselves and their employees. From that point on, employers—depending on size—were required to include their workers in any retirement plan that gave the company a tax break. To add teeth, the IRS spelled out the rules for standardized plans. Since then, the public and private sectors have continued to develop a wide variety of benefit plans. Instead of learning about them all, we'll focus on basic plan concepts and introduce you to some of the most common names. Your HR rep will go over the one your employer has chosen. All are derived from alphanumeric sections of IRS law. For example, a share of employees in public education have a plan called the 403(b), and many state and local government personnel enroll in their 457(b). In the private sector, the most common plan currently is the 401(k). You've probably heard of that. Additionally, the private sector has several types of profit-sharing plans.

The biggest thing to know is that all plans are divided into two distinctly different types. One produces a lifetime payment; the other does not. Considering the implications, do you want what's behind curtain number one, or curtain number two?

Before we go there, you need to know the two ERISA tax advantages they share. First, contributions into any tax-qualified plan are excluded from your annual taxable income. If you were to put in a mere 5 percent of a $30,000 salary, for example, the IRS would assess payroll tax as if you were only earning $28,500. The upshot is that your tax bill decreases and your take-home pay increases—relatively speaking. Your money enters the plan by taking it out before your payroll check is cut. This is known as paying on a **pre-tax basis**. Second, earnings on those contributions are tax-deferred, and thereby remain in your plan, generating more profit. This interest on interest is called **compound interest**, which adds extra layers as the snowball rolls downhill. If you elect other benefits, like vision and dental coverage, your employer will subtract those premiums from your check after taxes have been withheld. This convenient way of purchasing is the **post-tax basis**.

Something psychologically interesting happens with all payroll deductions: *You never miss what you don't see.* As paydays roll by, you get used to running your budget on net pay.

You can withdraw tax-qualified money by simply asking, but currently Uncle Sam imposes a 10 percent penalty if you do so before age 59½. That becomes an issue for young men and women who elect to maximize their contributions from the giddyap. Some big expense always seems to come up, and they need the money back. Luckily, their plan might have the optional penalty-free borrowing provision. The IRS restricts loans to less than half your account value and must be repaid on an uninterrupted quarterly basis within five years. If the loan-repayment terms aren't met, the borrowed money becomes immediately taxable and a penalty is assessed.

With that said, we can get back to the two quite different overarching types of work-savings plans—the defined benefit plan, and the defined contribution plan.

The Defined Benefit Plan

A **defined benefit plan** produces a level monthly payment until you go to your just reward, although the plan may adjust up for inflation. It's an annuity, in the sense that it's a series of payments. In some cases, you can opt for a reduced lump sum, much like a lottery winner can take. These **pension plans** are funded by your employer (though many plans allow/require you to contribute, as well). Only a percentage of companies fully fund them. Some insure them. Those with partially funded plans list the unfunded portion as a liability on their balance sheet. It's an IOU. Financially strong companies can honor their commitments, but some companies have gone under and taken the pension funds with them. Search "pension fund collapse" to read about actual events or the looming threat for others.

What is "defined" in a defined benefit plan is the payout formula. In general, it comprises the number of years of your uninterrupted service and your average ending salary during some final segment of employment. The plan description sets out the length of time you need to work until you qualify for benefits, and how old you must be before payments can begin.

I'll illustrate one such defined benefit plan from the workplace. Suppose that your friend Archibald is employed by a company whose plan specifies that he will:

- earn 1 percent of his average salary during the last five years for every year of dedicated service . . .
- to become eligible to receive full benefits at age fifty-five, and
- must work thirty years to qualify for full benefits.

In this case, if Archie started working for the company at age twenty-five and wanted to retire thirty years hence, and his closing monthly salary averaged $5,000 during the last five years, his monthly pension would be $1,500 (30 yrs. x $5,000 x 1% = $1,500). If he separates from employment before qualifying for even a partial benefit (that number of years will be stated in his plan document), Archie's potential dollars will stay in the employer's collective pot. However, Archie can withdraw any contributions that he made. Separation from employment may, or may not, be voluntary—much less justifiable or fair. That can be a pretty expensive issue if you quit, get fired, or are laid off just prior to qualification.

Many unions, railroads, governments, and their agencies have historically utilized defined benefit plans, and details vary by company within the same industry. A growing percentage of businesses have been phasing them out and are opting for the next type.

The Defined Contribution Plan

The **defined contribution plan** is recent by comparison and has evolved from the way many people now work—they change horses in the middle of the stream. This behavior excludes career hoppers from qualifying for pensions because they don't stay in one saddle long enough.

A significant difference between the defined benefit plan and the defined contribution plan is who funds it. In a defined contribution plan, it's up to you, not your employer, to set the money aside. What's "defined" is how much you authorize the employer to withhold from your check. However, ERISA permits your employer to contribute, as well. That helps.

Your defined contribution plan is portable. When you change employers, you can take your tax-qualified money with you. This nifty feature allows you to theoretically work for six different employers, for five years at a time each, and consolidate all contributions and earnings. Then you'll have structured your own thirty-year pension plan—assuming that each of the six employers sponsors this plan type. But you won't know what its future monthly benefit will be because there are too many variables. The potential payout will eventually be determined by your contributions, their timing, and the returns they enjoy. You can, of course, construct it to hit a targeted sum, such as that $1,500 of Archie's; we'll get back to that momentarily. But let's first look at a 401(k)—the most common defined contribution plan.

The IRS sets a limit on how much you can contribute annually to a 401(k). As a reference point, that dollar amount was $18,500 in 2018—which should seem meaningless to you. What's important is that your employer can also contribute via a matching feature—only if it wants to. That percentage is entirely on the company owner, who won't kick in anything if you don't participate.

Here's an actual example: Your employer offers to match 50 percent of your contributions up through 5 percent of your annual earnings. If your annual salary happens to be $30,000, then you would contribute $125 per month to max-out the benefit, and the company would kick in half that, or about $63 per month. That's what it budgeted for monthly when it hired you. Those are your dollars lying on the table, and they're gone for good if you don't pick them up. If you want every last dime, elect to contribute at the maximum matching rate they offer. In terms of profit, that decision amounts to a 100 percent return on investment. Where else can you get that?

There is a slight catch: Employer contributions aren't entirely yours until you become fully vested. **Vesting** requires a number of years of uninterrupted employment—commonly five. When that's the case, most plans vest by 20 percent annually, starting with the first year. An alternate vesting schedule makes you wait until the very last day of the fifth year. This is **cliff vesting**. Regardless of method, once you're fully vested, all previous and future company match money is yours to keep forever. But you may forfeit some, if not all, of your matched company money if you leave before becoming fully vested. Be that as it may, you can always move your contribution dollars to your next employer's plan.

Investment Choices

Your employer hires a plan administrator to provide investment choices and to handle questions and the plan mechanics. Typically, this third party offers a choice of at least four mutual fund types. These are often class "C" shares, which don't assess a sales charge. They are no-load funds.

- **Money market funds.** Your principal has virtually no risk to principal in money market funds. The rate of return will be low, but this is a good place to park contributions during times of indecision. If prevailing interest rates begin to rise, it may be wise to shift some dollars here and catch the wave.

- **Stock funds.** The opportunity for higher gains dwells in stock funds, but it's the most aggressive in terms of risk. Values can rise and fall both sharply and quickly. Stocks of old established companies are less volatile than most young ones. The selection may include growth stocks, dividends stocks, and a few that are considered undervalued. Equities have experienced a better return than most other investments over the long term.

- **Bond funds.** Corporate, government, and municipal bonds make up a bond fund. Returns will stay in the modest range, and values will fluctuate slowly. If prevailing interest rates start falling from their highs, this fund will rise in value automatically. If that's the case, shift some dollars here—especially those in your above money market fund.

- **Balanced funds.** These have a mix of stocks and bonds. This tends to keep the value of the fund more stable and should reduce risk from falling stock prices. The bond mix, though, hinders growth when interest rates are rising.

I can't tell you which curtain to choose, nor do I know of any study showing that companies offering a defined contribution plan pay more than those offering a pension plan. Each arrangement has its advantages and disadvantages, and you might not have much choice in the matter, anyhow. It's best to pursue a career based on your talents, interest, and motivation, instead of on which type of retirement plan an employer offers.

Let's return to that $1,500/month target we were talking about earlier and see how much it would take in a defined contribution plan, such as a 401(k), to crank out $1,500 per month as does Archie's defined benefit plan. To make things easy, I'll give you the formula and solve for

X, which is your nest egg (or stool leg, if you'd rather). In it, I'm using an annual **return on investment (ROI)** of 5 percent.

$$Monthly\ pension = \frac{(X)(ROI)}{12}$$

$$\$1,500 = \frac{(\$360,000)(5\%)}{12}$$

The equation indicates that you will need $360,000 thirty years from now. To reach that number, you'll need to have contributions of $12,000 per year, or $1,000 per month for thirty years. You can start next week.

Don't freak out and close the book! Stick with me, and I'll show you how to turn a battleship around in a bathtub.

In the first place, you're seven or more years younger than Archie. These extra years make your monthly contribution drop to $662. ("Big deal," I hear you say.) What's more, you may have been so shocked that you forgot that your dollars are going to be invested and will yield earnings. It's not like you'll be sticking money in a backyard coffee can for all those years. Plus, the compound returns you'll receive, along with tax-deferred interest, will further add to your nest egg, thus reducing contributions even more. Not only that, remember that your employer will probably be kicking in money, too. Feel better?

"Just how low can I go, dude? My pockets are nearly empty, as it is."

It can be astonishingly low, my friend. The answer lies in your budget and the time value of money. The table shown in Figure 10-1 illustrates this crucial concept graphically. An annuity, as you recall, is a series of payments. An "annuity due" indicates the payments are made at the beginning of a period, just as rent is due on the first.

Let's look at some possibilities. Suppose that you decide to invest $600 on the first of June each year, and title the account "Nest Egg." The money could come from an annual tax refund or from saving

	1.0%	3.0%	5.0%	8.0%	10.0%	12.0%
Year						
1	1.01000	1.03000	1.05000	1.08000	1.10000	1.12000
2	2.03010	2.09090	2.15250	2.24640	2.31000	2.37440
3	3.06040	3.18363	3.31013	3.50611	3.64100	3.77933
4	4.10101	4.30914	4.52563	4.8666	5.10510	5.35285
5	5.15202	5.46841	5.80191	6.33593	6.71561	7.11519
6	6.21354	6.66246	7.14201	7.9288	8.48717	9.08901
7	7.28567	7.89234	8.54911	9.636683	10.43589	11.29969
8	8.36583	9.15911	10.02656	11.48756	12.57948	13.77566
9	9.46221	10.46388	11.57789	13.48656	14.93742	16.54874
10	10.56668	11.8078	13.20679	15.64549	17.53117	19.65458
20	22.23919	27.6764	34.71920	49.42292	63.00250	80.69874
40	46.79483	77.6633	126.8393	279.781	486.85180	859.1424
50	60.84721	116.1808	219.8154	619.6718	1280.299	2688.02

Figure 10-1   Future Value of an Annuity Due

$50 each month for a year. That's approximately $1.65/day, which is lower than most beverages and is exceedingly less than a $10 pack of cigarettes. (In thirty years, you would have burned up $109,500 if you smoked a pack a day!) Now let's say that you chose to invest that $600 annually in a 1 percent savings account. What would it be worth in four years? Go to the Annuity Due table and find the multiplier that sits at the intersection of the 1 percent column and the year-four row, which is 4.10101, and highlighted in green. By multiplying this by $600, you get $2,460.06.

But what if you could get 5 percent return somewhere else? Go back to the table and multiply $600 by 4.52563, which is shown in green under the 5 percent column. That gives you $2,715.38, which is a mere ten percent more in value. Now try $600/year at 5 percent for fifty years. You would have $131,889.24. And at 12 percent (shown in yellow), you'd be a millionaire with $1,612,812.26! Try any combination of investment, number of years, and return you'd like.

Study this table for a second. See how the returns just absolutely skyrocket in the late years, and are further magnified by an increased **return on investment** (ROI). This is the **time value of money**! Its implications are ginormous:

- The earlier you begin, the less you have to save later. Buy and hold—for decades—just like the professionals, adjusting only when necessary.

- You can achieve equal or better results by investing and holding in a quality account with a lower ROI (take less risk) than investors who starts late and have to achieve big returns, which come with more risks. They're the late ones seeking investment advice online and in the *Wall Street Journal*, trying to catch up for lost time.

Let's talk about this "catch-up" for a moment more. As I'm trying to indicate above, some adults get hung up on trying to move money around to catch an extra half or quarter point of interest. You can outdo any of them today by simply choosing not to spend a twenty-dollar bill once a month and, instead, putting that Andrew Jackson into savings. That's the same as the profit-in-hand that your business would earn monthly on an imaginary twelve thousand dollars at 2 percent!

$$\underline{\$12,000 \ (.02)} = \frac{\$20}{12}$$

A rate chaser, on the other hand, would have to possess this principal amount and move it to a higher risk spot to match you.

Moreover, if your investment is in a tax-qualified plan at work or home, the compound interest effect doesn't get wrecked. But, as you'll hear me say time and again, don't overcontribute to qualified savings plans during your early years. Getting money out for emergencies causes penalties and taxes.

And as they say on TV, "Wait! We're not done yet!" By the time you reach your mid-fifties, you're in your prime earning years, and the big expenses of raising a family should be behind you. This combination of higher income and lower expenses will allow you to do even better by dedicating larger monthly contributions to X. I know of couples who are socking away better than $1,000 per month right now without blinking an eye.

Now, let's go back to that $360,000 conundrum, and work on a solution from a different angle. If we raise the ROI by just 1 percent, the nest egg needed drops to $300,000—which is 17 percent less. Accordingly, it makes sense that, during your saving years, you want to earn a high ROI on your contributions. Cumulatively, you won't have to contribute as much. Conversely, if the ROI drops to 4 percent, X increases to $450,000, which means that you must contribute 25 percent more to reach the same $1,500 benefit.

A hardworking ROI requires an investment in equities, such as domestic and international stocks, real estate limited partnerships funds, precious metals funds, stocks of emerging markets (the developing world), technology stocks (you can guess at many of these these companies), **large cap stocks** (industry slang for its capitalization size), **small caps**, etc. Perform an Internet search for any or all categories to bring up relatable examples of these **growth stocks**. You can temper your risk by diversifying into bonds (medium ROI), but if you put all your money in low-risk savings, like money markets (low ROI), you're almost sure to come up short. And keep in mind that $1,500 is just arbitrary. Toggling the future benefit up will necessitate an increase to X, which means additional saving and/or a higher ROI. Committing too much to high-ROI investments broadens your risk exposure because high rates of return aren't consistently sustainable. Making the pursuit of riches a false god is one of the devil's favorite tricks.

Some disciplined combination is going to work for you, and you have plenty of years ahead to do formal financial planning. Realize also that X will deplete as you make withdrawals. Fortunately, you'll find more solace in your stool's third leg—savings plans at home.

Savings Plans at Home

It won't take long to realize that X won't be your only asset to work with late in life. Cash value in a life policy or annuity is an example—perhaps even a brokerage account. So is the equity in a big house that you probably won't need. These are all part of your stool's third leg; they're components of your total net worth, which we'll focus on in Chapter 12. We'll wrap up this chapter by making you comfortable with an IRA.

Individual Retirement Account

Congress created the **Individual Retirement Account**, or IRA, as part of ERISA. As implied, it is a long-term savings plan that you own and control—lock, stock, and barrel. It too is a defined contribution plan like the big boys. Creating a traditional IRA fills the need for the following three scenarios:

- It serves as a tax-qualified investment vehicle for self-employed people. An IRA has a lower IRS-contribution limit than a 401(k). The most you could contribute for 2018 was $5,500. Aside from that, it features the same tax deferrals and withdrawal penalties.

- It serves as a supplementary plan for employed people whose pension plans or contribution plans won't be enough to secure them later. You can simultaneously have an IRA and an employer-sponsored plan.

- It serves as a haven for tax-qualified distributions from employer-sponsored plans. If you separate from an employer with a defined contribution plan and hire on with an employer that doesn't sponsor one, you'll need a tax-qualified place to stash the accumulated contributions you leave with. If you cash them out, they become taxable income and come with penalties. Put that money into a **rollover IRA**, which is specifically designed to accept savings-plan distributions. Your previous employer will forward your rollover money after you set up an account. You can simultaneously have a regular IRA and a rollover IRA, and still participate in a qualified plan at work.

There are other IRA types that serve specific needs, including the **Roth**, which uses after-tax dollars that can be withdrawn. Facetiously, it can double as a bandage for people who don't know how to budget or who have waited too long to get started. Eventually, you might become skilled enough to establish a **self-directed IRA** within a tax-qualified brokerage account. A self-directed IRA can also house valuable artwork, gold, and other unique appreciable assets. All the facts about IRA variations are contained in the mandatory booklet that comes with your account. Your banker might readily give you a complimentary copy of the IRA booklet or search "IRA" at the IRS website. Consider either an advance peek. Setting up an IRA is off limits until you're working full time and have your other ducks in a row.

Establishing Your IRA

When you are ready, creating an IRA is nothing more than the stroke of a pen in the correct box of a standard account application. You can set one up at your bank or credit union. Each has the enrollment kits, and each has specially designed accounts for people just starting out. The institution you choose will be designated as your IRA custodian and, as such, will handle the mandatory IRS reporting for a nominal annual fee. Funding an IRA can be quite inexpensive. Opening balances at banks and credit unions have low minimums, and additions can go in anytime, no matter how small. Save your spare change each month, and toss it in. With higher opening deposits, you can get into a CD or a government bond. Once you've saved enough to meet the minimum for a securities investment, transfer your money into a mutual fund, for example, to gain a potentially higher return. If such isn't available at the bank or credit union, a local financial planner will help. You can also contact any mutual fund investment company.

Now you have all three legs of your stool. The longer they are, the higher you'll sit. If one is short, it'll be wobbly. If one is missing, you'll have one heck of a time. If you simply start with the minimums at work and home, you're poised to be sitting pretty. At your age, you don't have to develop a full-blown financial plan covering your lifetime— nor should you try, right now. Steady drops from your income stream into a well-formulated budget that will, amazingly, start floating your battleship.

In review, here are points to remember:

- Sign up at the maximum matching level, so those free dollars don't get away.
- The earlier you begin working toward X, the less you'll need to contribute to any of your plans on a regular basis.
- The farther out you peg your retirement age, the more time you have to build your stool.
- The higher the ROI you receive, the less you have to contribute.
- As you grow older, begin moving out of higher-risk equities and into safer government bonds; municipals (to save on taxes); utility and income stocks; and CDs.

You can frame this philosophy.

Helpful Link

2018 Social Security trust fund report

https://www.ssa.gov/policy/trust-funds-summary.html

Chapter 11

FORMULATING YOUR BUDGET

The word *budget* feels misunderstood and underappreciated. It whines, for instance, when it hears someone answer, "I can't afford to go to New York with you. I live on a budget." Before it develops an inferiority complex, I suggest that it should simply overlook the unintentional rap, if all the person meant to say was that money was too tight. On the other hand, I most certainly agree that there's cause for concern when a person views their finances from the subordinate side of a master/servant relationship. After all, who's in charge here?

Perhaps its cause for distress stems from the fact that the word *budget* is an intangible, which you can't see or touch. To complicate matters, it has both a verb and noun form. In verb form, to budget means to spend down income. In noun form, it's the distribution arm of your financial structure. With that reality, you can see that we all live on a budget—even billionaires. But billionaires don't have to operate under battle conditions like you do.

Our objective here is to assess this part of your financial structure, just as you would first check out a swing—another tangible that has a noun and verb form—but not the mental hang-up. Either way, it's best do an inspection to avoid landing on your back pockets.

Events can happen quickly. If parents give Jacinta an allowance to spend in a candy store, she might run through it in a matter of seconds—or, she might spend only half and pocket the difference. It all depends on her priorities. Then again, she might be in such awe of a bounteous selection that she has trouble making up her mind. The Cheshire Cat, in Disney's original animated feature *Alice in Wonderland,* knew all about objectives and decisiveness. When he asked Alice where she wants "to get to" in her adventure of chasing the White Rabbit, she starts to answer with, "It really doesn't matter, just. . . ." Before she can finish, he interrupts her: "Then it doesn't really matter which way you go." So it is with budgeting. Without an objective, then it doesn't really matter how you spend your money.

In this chapter, we won't spend any time discussing income, other than to reaffirm that its level is most often a function of education, which is one of the principal measurements of your value to society. We're here to formulate a budget that actually accomplishes something. For a professional lesson, we'll sit in on an educator's class as he focuses juniors and seniors on personal expenses and presents them with a standardized budgeting format. I'll add some commentary, and you can choose the goals.

The Budget's Elements

"Hello, class. My name is Mr. Johnson. Your budget has three types of expenses. For our purposes, I've adapted expense definitions from my accounting textbook to help you appreciate the differences. For our purposes, **fixed expenses** are necessary obligations that have both constant dollar amounts and monthly due dates. Relevant examples are contractual costs associated with staying connected to social media, such as phone and Internet bills. Other suitables include rent, car, and mortgage payments. (However, you might pay some fixed items quarterly or semiannually, such as car premiums.) Once you contract for goods or services, they become fixed expenses. If any payment is optional, it isn't an obligation. If it shows up on your credit report, you can be sure it's an obligation.

"Fixed expenses don't necessarily involve a contract. Should your health require insulin, then your prescription becomes a fixed cost. The necessity of riding the city bus five days a week makes that fare a fixed expense, too. Once you say 'I do,' you have no control over fixed costs until the obligations are fully met or canceled. In essence, a fixed expense is whatever is absolutely essential to running your life.

"**Variable expenses** are necessary expenditures associated with life but differ from fixed in the sense that their costs fluctuate with value selection and vary with levels of consumption. Food is a perfect example. You can learn to shop, cook, and feed yourself, or you can dine at Maury's Steak House seven days a week. You may have no control over gasoline prices, but a nonaggressive style of driving will yield higher fuel mileage. Then too, you can save on electricity by turning the lights out when you leave and by pulling on a sweatshirt, instead of cranking up the heat. Variable expenses don't always show up monthly—like sporadic purchases of clothing and footwear," Mr. Johnson explained.

About that time Hermione, the class history buff, volunteered: "Imelda Marcos must have been a lousy budgeter. After she and her husband Ferdinand abruptly fled power in the Philippines, those who forced them out were said to have discovered more than a thousand pairs of shoes in her closet, a trove of mink coats, and countless handbags. That woman must have shopped all the time!"

"Indeed, young lady," Mr. J. said. "There are many lessons to be learned from that story. My point is you have a ton of control over what and how much you spend on variable expenses.

"**Discretionary expenses**," our instructor went on to say, "are costs unassociated with survival. Music, artwork, and entertainment make perfect matches. You have complete control over these costs."

When Justin told on himself by saying, "I just can't live without my phone," the prof charitably conceded that differentiating between variable and discretionary expenses takes a bit of thinking.

"To see if you're getting the idea," Mr. Johnson said, as he started passing out papers, "mentally choose which items fall under each of the three expense categories on this handout. Afterward, I'll have you write out a list of how you actually spend your money. That's the first step in budgeting. Go ahead. I'll wait."

Remarkably Common Expenses

Club memberships	Hobbies	Fashion clothes
Alms/handouts	School supplies	Music downloads
Tech devices	Sporting events	Savings accounts
Cellular contracts	Internet contracts	Music lessons
Junk food	Parking	Parking tickets
Laundry/dry cleaning	Church offerings	Car washes
Movies	Christmas gifts	Pet food
Orthodontics	Glasses/contacts	Doctor and dental costs
Personal hygiene	Haircuts	Nails/manicures
Car insurance	Life insurance	Renters insurance

Figure 11-1   Mr. Johnson's Remarkably Common Expenses List

Using figure 11-1 as a mental prompt, complete this first step by jotting down your own expenses on tear-out 2, in the back of the book. (You can also use the following sample [figure 11-2].) Don't worry about assigning dollar amounts just yet.

The Budget's Format

When finished, you're ready for Professor Johnson's second step. He asserts that your budget's mathematical structure must be consistent with GAAP. The civilized world works by these rules, so this exercise will get you in step. Figure 11-3 contains the basic format, along with Mr. Johnson's notations. Transfer your categorized-expense list to tear-out 3 in the back of the book; add rows, if necessary.

Now's the time to assign costs and do the math. The bottom line tells you how well you're running the business of your life. If "Unspent Money" is a negative number, don't despair. The emerging picture is only a snapshot in time. Next month's go-around will likely be different

Budget Formulation's First Step

Fixed Expenses

_____

_____

_____

_____

Variable Expenses

_____

_____

_____

_____

Discretionary Expenses

_____

_____

_____

_____

Figure 11-2   Budget Formulation—Step One

and, in six months, side-by-side comparisons will make you laugh, cry, or beam with pride.

You may realize that you don't know the cost of items your folks are paying for—such as orthodontics and glasses—but are quite personal to you, and which you'll have to assume at some point. This is a good time to ask Mom or Dad questions, or do some Internet research on these and other future costs. For instance, do you know what it costs for parking in front of a fire hydrant or getting a speeding ticket? Perhaps more importantly, do you realize what a moving violation or a careless driving ticket does to your liability insurance rate? If no one's told you already, it boosts

Budget Formulation, Step Two

Name _____

Budget for the month of _____

Income

Wages/tips/salary $ _____

Allowance   (If you have one)   _____

Other   (Odd jobs, gifts, etc.)   _____

Total Income $ _____

Expenses

Fixed (in order of importance)

_____ $ _____

_____   _____

_____   _____

Variable (in order of importance)

_____ $ _____

_____   _____

_____   _____

_____   _____

Discretionary (most common to least)

_____   _____

_____   _____

_____   _____

_____   _____

Total Expenses $ _____

Unspent Money $ _____

(Subtract your totals, and there you have it.)

Figure 11-3   Budget Formulation—Step Two

it by hundreds of dollars a month for years to come. That scenario wreaks total havoc on your budget and scuttles your carefully laid plans.

And from now on, neatness counts. You can pick up an inexpensive columnar pad at any office-supply store and create monthly budgets for a couple of years. If you have Microsoft Excel, which is based on the ancient columnar pad, set yourself up on that software. At this point it's probably a waste of money to buy budgeting software, such as Quicken. Later, yes. The same holds true with downloadable budgeting apps. The secret to success is being well skilled at the task—not wielding the flashy tools.

For step three, we're back in Mr. Johnson's next session, learning about a spreadsheet that helps you budget accurately, both now and in the future.

"Welcome back," Mr. J. says with a smile. "In order to sharpen their budgeting skills, accountants created a worksheet, consisting of rows for income and expenses, and columns for projections and actual results. These professionals titled it the **monthly budget forecast**. Then, the bean counters plugged in the associated data and crunched the numbers to see how their estimates compared with reality. Successful budget managers made appropriate adjustments and went from there. Your assignment," Mr. Johnson continues, "will be to create your personal monthly budget forecast, using the same format that Luke did during last semester. Here's a copy he said we could use.

"Under the Forecast column in the Income portion, Luke estimated his part-time earnings and included them with the $250 his folks gave him monthly to cover expenses as he saw fit. He also plugged in a few extra bucks for doing odd jobs," our instructor adds. "In the Forecast column of the Expense portion, he entered the money order for $89, which his dad wanted back for signing his phone-carrier contract. That was his sole fixed expense—indicated by placement. Best guesses at variable costs followed, with 'Other' representing discretionary spending. At the end of the month, he recorded his receipts under the Actual header, and, as you see, came in under total budget, even though he

Monthly Budget Forecast Luke LeDuc For the Month of _____			
	Forecast	**Actual**	**Difference**
Income			
Take home pay	$310	$342	$32
Allowance	250	250	0
Miscellaneous	50	0	– 50
Total Projected Income	$610	$592	($18)
Expenses			
Bundled Internet and phone	$89	$89	$0
Meals out	60	47	13
Clothing	65	92	– 27
Entertainment	30	44	– 14
Books and school supplies	25	30	– 5
Personal grooming	40	24	16
Gifts	20	0	20
Local transit fares	100	84	16
Dating	100	68	32
Other	31	70	– 39
Total Projected Expenses	$560	$548	$12

Figure 11-4   Monthly Budget Forecast

overspent in four areas and underestimated total income. It's nicely done. I gave him a B.

"One shot at forecasting won't cut it because month-to-month income and expenses for juniors and seniors can fluctuate wildly—as does income. In time, the worksheet exercise won't look like seismo- graph readings during an earthquake, but, before that happens, you may have to carry things over to the next columnar sheet. Eventually you'll have a stable budget; the intangible will become tangible."

Figure 11-5 is a budget forecast worksheet, complete with a cash flow analysis section. To incorporate this feature into the Forecast portion, move any January net income—or loss—to the "Cash flow carryover (C)" line in the February forecast, and so on. (Again, you'll find a forecast-worksheet tear-out in back [#4].) You can extend this matrix right for quite a while—either in Excel or on extra pages of a wide columnar pad. Eventually, as the instructor says, your budget won't change much, month to month. After that you can drop back to a single month preparation. You'll see a well-formulated one in the next chapter.

Before Mr. Johnson dismisses class, he will give some operational tips from the workplace. But before we come back to that, let's talk a little about what it takes to manage finances each month.

The Personal Finance Management Cycle

I hear that you have enough money to pay the entire year's rent in January or prepay any number of your bills. Nice. The rest of us are stuck in a monthly earning and spending pattern. This is our personal finance management cycle. We try paying our bills in the order of fixed, variable, and discretionary, but life seems to get in the way. Occasionally, one is paid late, or another slips the mind entirely. And those late charges! They seem like such cruel punishment. What's worse is that tardiness goes on our credit report for seven years. To lend flexibility to your management cycle, spread out due dates when you can. Some merchants and service providers allow you to pick a specific payment date.

Corporate budget managers make it easy on themselves by maintaining a file labeled "payment control." It contains an updated list of every fixed company expense. When each month begins, they prepare all those checks and release them by due date and available funds. Create your own payment control system by doing the same. Yours might include register entries at the beginning of each month for all automatic

Budget Forecast Worksheet

	January Forecast	Actual Results	Difference	February Forecast	Actual Results	Difference	March Forecast	Actual Results	Difference
Income									
Take-home pay	$___	$___	$___	$___	$___	$___	$___	$___	$___
Monthly Allowance	___	___	___	___	___	___	___	___	___
Miscellaneous	___	___	___	___	___	___	___	___	___
Cash flow carryover (C)	___	___	___	___	___	___	___	___	___
Total (A)	$___	$___	$___	$___	$___	$___	$___	$___	$___
Expenses									
	___	___	___	___	___	___	___	___	___
	___	___	___	___	___	___	___	___	___
	___	___	___	___	___	___	___	___	___
	___	___	___	___	___	___	___	___	___
	___	___	___	___	___	___	___	___	___
	___	___	___	___	___	___	___	___	___
Total (B)	0	$___	$___	$___	$___	$___	$___	$___	$___
Cash Flow Analysis									
Income total (A)	$___	$___	$___	$___	$___	$___	$___	$___	$___
Subtract Expense total (B)	___	$___	$___	$___	$___	$___	$___	$___	$___
Net income (loss) moves up to the carryover line (C) for next month	$___	$___	$___	$___	$___	$___	$___	$___	$___

Figure 11-5   Budget Forecast Worksheet

payments and account-maintenance fees. Strike a balance afterward to see how much you have to work with.

Another good habit is training yourself to make debit-card entries as soon as possible.

String up a safety net, while you're at it. Accountants call this best friend of neutral gender **working capital**. It's a mini-cash-reserve that businesses maintain in their checkbook as a way of getting through lean weeks. They experience the same problems you do.

On a personal level, I knew of a guy who had a particularly difficult time of keeping an accurate balance and invariably received an NSF. One day, his wife deposited an extra $500 in their account without telling him or recording it in their register—making it invisible working capital. Months later, he proudly mentioned, "I'm doing much better, dear. I haven't bounced a check for quite a while." She smiled and gave him a peck on the cheek, knowing that he wouldn't find out because she was the one who reconciled their checkbook.

I don't know that trying to fool yourself is going to work. You're going to have to consciously make this shock absorber a permanent portion of your checkbook balance. The most practical way to acquire this first line of defense is buying it on monthly installments. In other words, slice a little here and there from your variable and discretionary spending, and let those shavings accumulate in your checkbook. Like any relationship, it takes time to build but, once you're married to it, it will stand in place with you for the rest of your life. If a whopper of an emergency strikes, fall back on your cash reserve, instead of wiping out your working capital. You wouldn't sell out a friend, would you?

As we rejoin our class, our teacher is commenting on a budget's bottom line:

"If your income and expenses run consistently near equal, your budget is taking on equilibrium. If expenses continue to exceed income, that's a different story. You'll have to come up with some combination of lower variables and fewer discretionary costs until it is. After all, you can't alter fixed line items."

"But, why?" Jablonski asked. "There's no law against an unbalanced budget, is there? Look at DC. Won't creative credit get me through until my income goes up?"

"It might, but how did a 'sophomore' get into my class? At any rate, discussions on the efficacy of deficit spending is for Mrs. Jacobs' economics class. I was just under the impression that you wanted to know when you can stand on your own two feet!"

As the bell rang, the kid's lights came on. In digesting Mr. Johnson's not-so-subtle remarks, he realized that the turning point for financial stability is when income consistently blows away expenses.

Some economists refer to what's left over as "disposable income." But is that terminology at all helpful? It's certainly accurate if you ride the consumerism bandwagon or believe that it's okay to waste this remainder. It's counterproductive if you feel that building wealth and reducing debt are superior principles. More reflective people define this overage as **discretionary income**, but both terms can leave you chasing white rabbits. I believe that **undirected income** hits the nail on the head. Now you've created something that stands there subserviently, waiting for you to decide what to do with it. There's also no discussion about who is master and who is servant.

You'll recall seeing "Unspent Money" as your bottom line in Figure 11-3. Forget that little trick. This terminology is better suited for eighth-graders. You now have the skill to classify expenses correctly, and can place them in format with income. You're equipped to move to the last formulation step—that of incorporating goals. If Luke would have worked this one into his budget forecast, Mr. Johnson would have given him an A.

Goals and Objectives

In time, you'll settle on any number of stated objectives—including farming land of your own, teaching at a college, or someday home-schooling children of your own. Who knows? Perhaps you'll aspire to be a concert pianist or a master electrician? None of these desires is accomplished through a one-step process but, is achieved by setting and meeting ordered goals. If you consider step 1(a) to be socking away $50 per month, from what other source of income would the dough come but your undirected income? You can get the ball rolling by erasing $50 worth of discretionary expenses and combining them on a line labeled, "Saving for my goal." You're free to dedicate more or fewer dollars, depending on your budget. As your income and resolve increase,

Source: Public Domain {PD-1923}

move the budget line item up through variable expenses and, finally, into fixed. Along the progression, be sure to deposit the seed money into an actual savings account to keep it from blurring with your working capital.

With the level of undirected income setting the bar height, near-term goals for the average junior or senior may suitably be new tech components or fashion ensembles. They might even include an unflashy set of snow tires or a metric wrench set. You have quite an assortment of essential items to accumulate before you feel well-equipped to set your sights on personal objectives.

The world is full of different Jacintas and Imeldas. Some will shop for Early American at fine-furniture stores, knowing that quality is remembered long after price is forgotten. Others will furnish their apartments with "Early Goodwill," knowing that they can buy good furniture when the kids aren't going to carve their initials on it. You'll set your goals based on your philosophy.

People of faith have found relevant guidance in the sixth chapter of Matthew. In particular, verses 19–21 and 25–33 give new meaning to the term "balanced budget." Within the Beatitudes—which Danish painter Carl Bloch portrayed most beautifully here—Jesus gives us clear direction for adopting an outlook on material goods and true riches, and bids us to trust in the Father, who knows that we have wants and needs, and who promises to provide. We shouldn't be amazed, then, when they come to us through prayer (Matt. 7:9–11), and as we dutifully work to provide and care for one another and for ourselves.

Helpful Link

Budgeting Software

https://www.quicken.com

Chapter 12

PERSONAL FINANCIAL STATEMENTS

If I could only write one chapter, this would be it. Personal financial statements are that important. These are your power tools, my friend. A full set of statements is comprised of the income and expense statement and the net worth statement.

Your **net worth statement** is the equivalent to Francisco's balance sheet, back in Chapter 8. He drew up a balance sheet to calculate the equity in his business. You'll discover your own net worth when you subtract what you owe from what you own. This document is a mile marker, which indicates where you are along the financial highway. When you compare bottom lines of consecutive preparations, the resultant change will tell you if you're still headed north or have looped back south.

A common detour on your journey is deficit spending, in which you finance your way down a narrow, winding road—using a credit card as a guardrail. You can avoid scraping your fender by instead making a steering correction to expenses. Not only will that maneuver keep you out of the ditch; it will give you better mileage out of your check.

Your **income and expense statement**, more commonly known simply as the income statement, shows your profit. It's like a speedometer, showing how fast you're traveling along the financial highway. How frequently you create the report will be a function of how important you consider the information. Business owners must pull one together quarterly to meet tax-reporting requirements. Doing so additionally gives owners and investors (if applicable) a reference point on how well the operation is performing. When Francisco compared consecutive quarterly reports, he could see either an expansion or contraction of his profits. You'll learn how to create and analyze these two powerful diagnostics as we study the financials of Brandon and Marie Thompson, a couple not much older than you.

The pair recently bought a house, replaced Marie's old clunker of a car, and were blessed with little Jennifer. We'll play detective, just as a loan officer would if he or she were to examine their personal statements. After all, your signature goes on the bottom line of a loan application, and a good loan officer must protect the bank—along with keeping your well-being in mind.

Brandon and Marie assembled their year-end statements in late January by emptying their bankers box and sorting last year's records and receipts in anticipation of filing their tax return. Moreover, they wanted to know where they stood, considering all the changes at home. Marie has been staying home with the baby, and the new parents want to decide how to handle Jennifer's care if and when Marie goes back to work. Day care costs can approximate what you earn in a month, thereby making that a wash.

The Net Worth Statement

To create your own net worth statement, list your assets in descending order by liquidity in the assets portion, and arrange your obligations in the liabilities section by how quickly you expect to pay them off—or to be **amortized**. The Thompsons' document is illustrated below in Figure 12-1.

Brandon and Marie's liquid assets, such as cash reserves, are shown in green, and less liquid ones are in blue. By the time we're finished, you'll see why differentiating assets and expense types on financial statements is so important. Their home-furnishings category is made up of durable goods, such as appliances and fine furniture. Marie's SUV entry stands by itself because of its corresponding entry in the

Statement of Net Worth Brandon and Marie Thompson For year ended 12/31/20__		
Assets		
Checking	$2,150	
Savings	6,397	
Certificate of Deposit	2,000	
Car goal (credit union account)	50	
EE savings bonds	1,200	
Life Insurance cash value	752	
Stock portfolio	1,784	
IRA (mutual funds)	3,112	
401(k) plans	2,808	
Home furnishings	2,900	
Automobiles	14,000	
Personal property	9,400	
Residence	196,000	
Total Assets		$242,553
Liabilities		
Credit card balance	$950	
Church pledge	5,000	
Student loans	9,140	
Car loan	12,000	
Home mortgage	176,400	
Total Liabilities		$203,490
Net Worth		$ 39,063

Figure 12-1   Statement of Net Worth

liabilities section. If they owned a valuable collector car, it too would have its own line; otherwise, paid-off cars of lower value are lumped in with personal property. Clothes, pots and pans, and fishing gear are of subjective value, and don't impact net worth, but are still listed as a barometer of spending. Last on the list is the couple's new home—their most expensive asset.

The Thompsons' liabilities are straightforward and don't need comment, with the exception of their church capital-contribution pledge. Because this isn't an enforceable obligation it doesn't have to appear on a statement, but in the interest of full disclosure, the couple decided to list that character statement.

When obligations are subtracted from assets, Brandon and Marie's net worth is just over $39,000—half of which is in the house. You can deduce that by comparing the home's recently appraised value to its listed mortgage balance. The $20,000 difference was likely their 10 percent down payment, and reflects their equity. This hefty percentage probably precluded them from having to take on the cost of private mortgage insurance, or PMI.

Playing Sherlock Holmes, you could gain even more insight. The Thompsons' seemingly modest credit card balance is not indicative of unrestrained spending, and the two loan balances seem manageable, considering the positive cash flow. Their credit report will show if they're telling the truth in detailing credit history—including particulars on their student loans, car loan, and new mortgage. In addition, their departmental-expense totals reveal that knocking out cash reserves and accumulating a house down payment were more important than buying furnishings and personal property. Long-term savings appear to take a backseat as well. Donning an analyst cap discloses by percentage what their categories are to section totals:

In the assets section:

• Cash reserves are just over 4%.
• Long-term savings are a mere 3.6%.

- The EE education bonds don't even register on the Richter scale.
- Personal property is at $26,300, coming in at about 11%.
- Real estate is a whopping 81% of the total.

In the liabilities section:

- Their credit card balance isn't even 1%.
- The church pledge is 2½%.
- Student loans stand at 4½%.
- Marie's car loan approaches 6%.
- Their mortgage is nearly 87% of what they owe.

A few probes might disclose their motivation to get into a house; if they had rented longer, they could have wiped out 74 percent of their liabilities with their down payment or possibly even purchased rental property. Maybe the housing market and financing climate were favorable, thereby leading them to buy. Other factors could have played a role as well—such as locating in a good school district or, moving closer to family or work. Let's not make an unproductive value judgment. We only hope that characters who don't have anything to do with earning their money or paying their bills didn't unduly influence them. Mortgage lenders, real estate agents, builders, and some policymakers in DC advance the idea that you should get into a house to achieve a big part of the so-called American dream—and pronto! They may be wanting to stimulate the economy, but is buying real estate always a worthwhile objective, and who are they to tell you what's best for you? If you're a renter and buy into their philosophy, then you risk viewing yourself as unfulfilled and inadequate—maybe even second-class. (Maybe more importantly, we wouldn't want to make a house an idol.)

While it's true that property has historically appreciated in value, the second decade of this century proved that there's significant vulnerability to real estate when prices advance too rapidly. When the economy's artificial housing bubble burst, national home prices plummeted, and borrowers who were unqualified in the first place lost their homes and ruined their credit in the landslide. That event is reminiscent of the tulip-bulb scandal in Holland centuries ago—only this time policy makers and groups with a vested interest were cheering on the hapless, unknowledgeable buyers.

Now, try your hand at creating your own net worth statement, using tear-out page [#5] from the back of the book. Or, do it on columnar

Net Worth Statement

Name _____

Date _____

Assets

_____ $_____

_____ _____

_____ _____

_____ _____

_____ _____

_____ _____

_____ _____

                   Total $ _____

Liabilities

_____ _____

_____ _____

_____ _____

_____ _____

_____ _____

                   Total $_____

                Net Worth $

Figure 12-2   Your New Worth Statement

paper or create it in Excel. Make it look as convincing as you can, despite the fact that most of what you might own is a wardrobe, smartphone, and tablet, with maybe some jewelry, watches, tools, and collectibles kicked in. Items you're on the hook for may be phone and Internet contracts and IOUs. Car loans, student loans, and credit card balances are added when you reach the legal age to assume them. Do the subtraction and tell yourself what you see. I won't look. I won't even ask if it's a positive number, but now you know what you're worth—at least in financial terms.

The Income Statement

Brandon and Marie stated their income and calculated their expenses in figure 12-3 below.

Their income entries don't need comment but, if they received large gifts or winnings, they should list this miscellaneous income to enhance their statement. The couple did include their tax refund, prompting them to remember how they spent it. As shown, their annual income totaled $61,498. Below that, Brandon and Marie recapped departmental spending. The green entries show how much they sent to short-term savings, while those in blue detail the amount they paid on obligations and placed in long-term savings. Red indicate their variable and discretionary expense totals.

Are the Thompsons such good record-keepers that they knew precisely what they spent in each department? I doubt it. Only cost accountants and near-obsessives do that. For instance, did they really spend exactly $7,200 on groceries and $600 on gifts? I asked Marie about it.

"We used to use three file jackets—marked Food, Clothing, and Shelter—and sorted afterward. History showed that we averaged $600 monthly on food. That's where the $7,200 came from. Costs like car insurance, utilities, and phone are easy to peg because there's just a handful of receipts. We also made some calculated guesses. However, now that finances have expanded, we budget on our PC. Because we're in a house we'll probably itemize next year. All in all, once our expenses

Statement of Income and Expenses Brandon and Marie Thompson Year End		
Income		
Brandon's wages (net)	$	30,540
Marie's wages (net)		29,016
Investment income		95
Tax Refund		1,847
Total		$ 61,498
Expenses		
Savings account	$	1,200
New car account		3,000
Jennifer's EE bonds		1,200
Life insurance premiums		1,320
Rent and mortgage payments		17,952
Car payments		1,650
Student loan payments		2,400
Credit card payments		3,418
IRA mutual funds		2,400
Clothes/other assets		1,950
Church offerings		2,160
Utilities		2,016
Cable and phone		1,987
Car Insurance		3,471
Groceries		7,200
Dry cleaning/laundry		84
Car maintenance/fuel		3,470
Personal care		1,416
Gifts		600
Dining & entertainment		1,560
Miscellaneous		1,044
Total		$ 61,498

Figure 12-3   Thompsons' Income & Expense Statement

and income stabilize we won't often prepare the formal statement, which mirrors our budget.

"And I'm happy to say," she continued, "that we've gone back to carrying sufficient cash because Brandon was tired of paying ATM charges. When he totaled them one year, he said we spent nearly enough to pay a month's rent. And we would never use a credit card for a cash advance. The interest rate it charges for that usage is over 25 percent! Maybe just as importantly, he quit letting an unfounded fear of getting mugged intimidate him."

When you add all outlays together, accounting principles dictate that their sum must match total income. That's not just for fun—it creates an equation that shows exactly where you spent your money, and in what amount. To make your two totals equal after you've plugged in costs from your receipts or records, you must add another expense line and fill in its dollar amount to make the upper and lower sections equal out. You can either title that entry "Miscellaneous," like the Thompsons did, or go with "I have no earthly idea how I spent this money!" Brandon and Marie were no exception and solved for X by process of elimination. With all their known expenses totaled and subtracted from income, the remaining $1,044 must have gone to double lattes, Powerball tickets, alms, and goofy stuff. That's less than three dollars per day.

Identifying impulse buying isn't the only lesson Brandon and Marie can learn—they can also see how categories of spending affect net worth. Every time they add to checking or savings, these outlays make a proportionately corresponding increase in the green section on their net worth statement, thus bumping up its bottom line. Activity in the blue section does the same, but in different ways and by differing amounts: Every time an IRA payment goes out, or they add to their portfolio, net worth can vary disproportionately. These securities are subject to market gyrations, which control both value's direction and velocity. Their life insurance premiums, on the other hand, have a built-in cost of insurance, so only a portion of the payment will reflect an increase in cash value. Their car, credit card and student-loan payments, are similarly offset by finance charges, thereby shrinking liabilities at a retarded rate. Their mortgage payment does the least to increase net worth. It makes the bottom line creep up at a snail's pace because early on, almost all of it consists of interest. House appreciation does help, but wardrobe, boats, furniture, and other personal assets—such as electronics and lawnmowers—depreciate as soon as you buy them.

As far as the red ones go, you can spend until you're blue in the face and never make an impact on your bottom line—they even don't show up on a net worth statement! Instead, these dollars simply trail off into the sunset, though they're predominately variable expenses.

Again, we look at category percentages to gain perspective on their spending:

- The green entries, totaling $4,200, indicate they saved just under 7% of income.
- Payments on their student loans, car loan, and credit cards total $7,468, and are 12% of outlay.
- Their IRA contributions and EE bonds represent nearly 6% of income.
- Life insurance premiums are slightly more than 2% of what they take home.
- The $1,950 labeled clothes, etc., barely exceeds 3% of spending.
- Their housing costs (a mixture of rent and house payments at that time) constitute just over 29%. There are also a few closing costs in the total, but the seller, in their case, paid the majority.
- The $25,008 they spent for other expenses is fractionally above 40% of total outlay.

Now you know where their priorities lie. If you ask whether these percentages fall within acceptable parameters, I would have to answer with a qualified yes. But don't get hung up learning rules of thumb. Of more benefit is calculating the percentages on your own statement. Figure 12-4 below is your opportunity to create one, using tear-out page 6. Afterward, ask yourself, "Does discretionary spending look too high? Are clothing costs higher because groceries are up? Am I saving even 1 percent of income? What portion is going toward my goals?"

Income and Expense Statement

Name _____

Period covered _____

Income

_____ $ _____

_____ _____

_____ _____

_____ _____

Total period income $ _____

Expenses

_____ $ _____

_____ _____

_____ _____

_____ _____

_____ _____

_____ _____

_____ _____

_____ _____

_____ _____

Total period expenses $ _____

Net income $ _____

Figure 12-4   Your Income & Expense Statement

Importantly, one percentage that contributes significantly to financial stability is that of monthly income to the mortgage payment. For decades after World War II, prime mortgage lenders and national policymakers said that they didn't want borrowers to put more than 25 percent of income into house payments. Much higher than that, and the numbers don't work. The paradigm worked pretty well, hence keeping foreclosure defaults low. How does Brandon and Marie's case compare? The Thompsons show their mortgage as $176,400. A thirty-year mortgage at 5 percent requires a $946.97 monthly **principal and interest** payment (**PI**). They're required to **escrow** (squirrel away) even more to cover annual **real estate taxes and property insurance** (**TI**). That could take several hundred more. For the sake of argument, let's add $300, and call their total mortgage payment (**PITI**) $1,246.97. When you multiply $4,963 (their combined take-home pay) by 25 percent, you get $1,240.75, which is within a few bucks of their payment. They appear to be on safe ground.

Brandon and Marie are in a good position to improve their net worth. One of the quickest ways to make it rise is to reduce debt. The couple will have their credit card debt wiped out before June at the rate they're paying, and can then shift additional payments to student loans or Marie's car note. The couple also learned that consistently adding extra to the principal section of their mortgage payment significantly shortens mortgage life and saves a ton of interest. But going overboard with it can run you short of working capital.

Maybe they'll tackle a new goal, like making home improvements. Maybe the baby will have other ideas. The young parents have to make room in the budget for diapers and assorted baby-related expenses. And weather extremes will affect their utilities estimate. Eventually, the two will address their church pledge. They could pay about $200 monthly or meet it annually with an anticipated tax refund.

After analyzing the Thompsons' expenses, I'll give you credit for recognizing the danger of dedicating too large a percentage of income to any one color. Bloating will either force something out of a balanced budget or lead to deficit spending, which beats the ever-living daylights out of net worth.

Assuming that their loan interest rates aren't out of whack, that the student loans aren't in default, and that they've been timely with all payments, would you advise giving them another loan, or are you starting to think they're overextending themselves? You can't be sure by what's on paper. Maybe there's a large salary increase coming. A good lender is going to learn as much as possible before extending cash, thereby serving everyone's best interest.

That hasn't always happened. As mentioned, mortgage defaults skyrocketed as we began the new century. That was due in part to the practice of qualifying borrowers without the due diligence called for in historically responsible lending. **Due diligence** is ensuring that all stipulated loan criteria satisfy the requirements put forth by the lender. That protects its shareholders. Congressional arm-twisting to get more people into houses, combined with the prospect of higher profits from the resulting mortgages, led some lenders to relax or bend the rules. In some cases, borrowers weren't even required to show proof of income and were allowed to assume mortgages that represented too large a portion of their income. Some lenders stacked these and other stinky mortgages and tied them with a pretty ribbon. In time, these packages entered the lending market, and were pawned off as good investments. Inspectors, in some cases, didn't practice due diligence, and let them slip through. Because a great many finance packages had little to no chance of working, the anticipated income never materialized for buyers, and the "house" of cards collapsed—taking with it billions of dollars and undermining the financial integrity of the country.

It has taken years for our economy to pull out of what some call the Great Recession—as if the economy's equalizing forces of supply and demand had mysteriously forgotten what they were supposed to do. What also may have been forgotten were the lessons to be learned from the Great Depression, which had its own roots in greed and a myopic view of regulation. These events bring to mind Aesop's fable of the dog crossing a bridge with a bone in his mouth. When he looked over and saw his reflection in the water, he opened up to snatch the prize from the other pooch . . . and lost his lunch.

The French have a term for government nonintervention in an economy: *laissez-faire*—meaning "hands off; let things be." You can search this term to get a background on this doctrine that developed in Europe some four hundred years ago. In theory this stance should work pretty well, but what all secular governments seem to have forgotten or ignored are the workings of the devil, who seeks to corrupt all noble ideals. Financial statements—which are an integral part of the country's economic stability—aren't exempt from his evil. Investors look to these documents for guidance, and society, as a whole, demands honesty and transparency within them. To that end, publicly owned companies must hire certified public accounting firms to audit their books for veracity and render opinions. When the numbers are all in, CPAs and company executives are required to sign off on the company's financial health. It is outrageous when top company executives disguise the truth. Personal greed, tempted by Satan, can strip people of their savings and destroy a company. When lies are exposed, federal regulators will, at the very least, impose fines. If gross malfeasance occurs, executives can go to prison if convicted. Furthermore, if it's proven that a public accounting firm is complicit in the action, the organization itself can suffer severe consequences. All of this has happened before.

But on a brighter and more optimistic note, you've learned a lot about every item listed on Brandon and Marie's statements. That knowledge and the skills you've learned within all the chapters put you at the pinnacle of readiness. You can now tell freshmen and sophomores that there are three effective strategies to increase their net worth:

1. Buy cash reserves and assets that appreciate in value.

2. Watch variable expenses, and curb discretionary spending.

3. Avoid unnecessary liabilities, and efficiently reduce the amount you do incur.

And don't forget to advise them to practice good risk management. Considering life's challenges, they should assess their financial exposure and insure what they can't afford to lose. Then too, counsel them to diversify their investments by holding different types of securities.

The first twelve chapters have been the meat and potatoes. I have added the following bankruptcy chapter as a bonus to tweak the big picture.

If you leave here: It's been my privilege to serve you. I wish you all success in running the business of your life.

Chapter 13

ALL ABOUT BANKRUPTCY

I wrote every other chapter to make this one of no personal relevance, despite the fact that I wasn't worried that you might fail. If I had not faith in you from the outset, I would have decorated it with yellow caution tape and placed it first. The content is included because a broad education in both secular and sacred matters is necessary to be an effective light. In the words of Rev. Rudolph G. Bandas, "Doubts against faith are due to ignorance, or carelessness in seeking the necessary information."[1]

Bankruptcy law is Christian faith in action. After all, we're to be more disposed to forgiveness and less inclined to lower the boom. This applies to not only personal relationships, but to the consequences of financial unpreparedness. Textbook examples of such are an inability to pay bills, exhausted lines of credit, and the consumption of remaining assets. In a word, such a person has become **insolvent**. Among other problems, that state leads to tunnel vision, an estimation of low self-worth, and a sense of hopelessness.

More often than you'd think, bankruptcy takes people by surprise. The insurmountable costs of uninsured medical attention will do the trick. Matters are worse if the injury or illness knocks them out of work, and they don't have disability insurance. Ultimately, their situation leads

---

[1] *The Cathedral Daily Missal*, 1961 (St. Paul, MN: E. M. Lohmann Company), 1903.

to filing bankruptcy, in a bid to gain relief—which is far better than holding up a liquor store.

Filing is a matter of public record, and there's no exception for notoriety. Do a search for "celebrity bankruptcies" to see some names. Fortunately, bankruptcies don't necessarily end careers by definition.

If you know someone whose financial life is going badly and projected to get worse, advise your friend to take a chair in an office of the **Consumer Credit Counseling Service**, or of another nonprofit with the same mission. This organization provides no-cost information about what can be done, and can help your pal develop a plan on ways to proceed. He or she will have to attend anyway, as counseling is a prerequisite to filing for bankruptcy. Going this route is superior to first spending money on a debt-consolidation program with a private company that advertises a cure-all. There are no quick fixes for dismal credit reports, regardless of what some advertising offers suggest. To quote the Federal Trade Commission, "No one can legally remove accurate and timely negative information from a credit report." Search "credit counseling" at your state's department of commerce website to bring up articles with more advice, and who to contact.

Once the decision to file has been made, conventional wisdom says stop making payments on debts you intend to include. Doing so won't hurt your case or cause more credit-report damage. All that continued payments do is consume what little cash you have left. And any encouragement from know-it-alls to run up credit card debt just prior to filing is bad advice. Action like that is out-and-out fraud. If the judge finds for it, and the amount is high, you could face both civil and criminal charges. If the violation isn't egregious, your case might still proceed, but those debts are likely to be excluded.

The act of filing a bankruptcy petition gets creditors off your back. This ends the relentless phone calls—often coming with unenforceable threats—because filing bars them from taking further action. Credit card issuers will, upon notification from the bankruptcy court, cancel your plastic.

If you wait too long to file, creditors can sue in civil court to force payment. Once you're in that spot, there'll likely be an unfavorable judgment if your only defense is a lack of funds. Creditors can then take that judgment and have your wages garnished—over and above having your bank accounts levied. Another creditor option is placing a lien on assets, like real estate. If the property is for sale, this title attachment will require satisfaction before ownership can change hands.

The petition must include all debts, both public and private. Once submitted, you can't amend the list, and you become fair game for omitted obligations. If you want to repay any debts after emerging from bankruptcy, you're certainly allowed to, but those payments are then considered to be gifts.

Local offices of the United States Bankruptcy Court adjudicate petitions along federal guidelines. However, many details and practices default to state's statutes. Because each state varies on how it handles assets, similar cases will produce different results in scattered parts of the country. Federal and state bankruptcy laws don't remain static, either. Congress significantly changed federal rules in October 2005, to make some debt forgiveness more difficult. The action was due in part to lobbying by unhappy creditors and to abuses by debtors.

You can either represent yourself in bankruptcy court, or hire an attorney. Do-it-yourself books are available at bookstores and online. Regardless of the route, there's a sizable federal filing fee.

Federal code has five filing types. For our purpose, we will discuss the three most common: Chapters 7, 11, and 13. Their differences amount to either straightening up a financial house, or knocking it down and starting it over.

Bankruptcy Types

Chapter 11 Bankruptcy

Reorganization is the operative word in Chapter 11 bankruptcy. It is intended for both small and large companies. They select this option to stay operating, while seeking the court's temporary protection. A court-appointed trustee then works with management and creditors, so business can proceed normally. These three players devise a restructuring plan that will allow the business to emerge as an ongoing concern, instead of selling off assets to pay debts.

Chapter 13 Bankruptcy

In Chapter 13 bankruptcy, families and individuals—rather than companies—are the beneficiaries of reorganization. Not many people qualify because of its high filing costs, attorney fees, and the limited amount of time afforded for resolution. Those who do make the cut generally have sufficient income, but are having a problem with maybe just one debt and will be able to move on after the issue is resolved. Falling behind with house payments is an example. Chapter 13 puts any foreclosure process on hold. Lenders may agree to a loan restructuring, which cannot last more than five years. If an affordable payment plan can be devised, the person or family's financial health can be restored; their home will be saved; and they can resume life as usual unless just one payment is missed. If that happens, the bankruptcy stands a high chance of being nullified.

Chapter 7 Bankruptcy

Chapter 7 bankruptcy is the liquidation form, and is designed to help insolvent individuals and families. Despite what you may have heard, filing for this version is not the same as scraping the paint off one's canvas and starting over debt-free. Rather, every nonexempt asset will be sold during the process, and proceeds will be used to pay at least something to creditors.

Federal bankruptcy law contains a list of assets that the government considers to be exempt from liquidation. States can adopt this liberalized list or elect to develop criteria of their own—which is the case about two-thirds of the time. Item inclusions vary notably from state to state. In some, Bibles are exempt—in other jurisdictions, they're not.

And nearly always, assets such as real estate require special handling. Historically, one of the most restrictive states has been Florida, where the exemption is a mere $1,000. That means things like clothes, furniture, toothbrushes, etc., are all subject to sale. It's likely that you will forfeit certain income streams like future sales commissions, too. On the other hand, some states are quite generous in deciding what can be kept. Many of them exempt food, clothing, household goods, wedding rings, burial plots, domestic animals, books, tools of trade, and automobiles up to a certain value.

On the court date, the bankruptcy judge examines the evidence, and—if approved—appoints a trustee to administer the case. Petitioners rarely, if ever, see the judge again. The trustee and the debtor meet afterward and settle on a dollar value of the nonexempt-asset list. From there, the filer decides whether to present such property for liquidation, or to redeem it with payments. When all proceeds are in, the trustee splits the money among the creditors, and sends the case back to the bankruptcy court. Upon satisfactory review, the judge orders the case closed. The discharge of allowable debts may come in just three months, but repayment to the trustee may take years, in some cases.

A variety of debts won't be forgiven, including court-ordered child support, alimony, and financial judgments stemming from personal injury or death to another. Neither will income taxes. If liquidation proceeds aren't enough to pay off Uncle Sam, the petitioner must devise a repayment schedule with the IRS—either through direct contact or with the aid of a tax attorney. Likewise with state taxes.

Student-loan balances won't make the cut, either. The only way out is proving hardship, which is difficult to do. Defaulters are aggressively pursued by collection agencies, which employ all legal methods of contact and persuasion—including wage garnishment. I should know—I was an agent for a short time.

If you owe on a federal student loan and are unemployed or earn very little, contact the loan originator, who can allow you to defer payments until you're on your feet. If your situation is chronic, take advantage of the **ICRP** program, which stands for **Income Contingent Repayment Plan**. Under this provision, all collection activity stops, and penalties and interest can sometimes be lowered substantially. You can stay in the program for decades, if necessary, because only an affordable percentage of your income needs to be applied to the defaulted student loan in question.

Your Credit Report

The world assesses your financial integrity by what it sees on your credit report. This document chronicles your borrowing and payment history, as well as listing liens, judgments, and any other legally reportable information about you. The oldest particulars—both good and bad—fall off within seven years. Consequently, your credit rating will eventually disappear if you don't engage with the world. Reportable items can include broken leases and evictions. The most dramatic one I witnessed was a team of Florida deputy sheriffs physically moving an apartment tenant and his contents onto the sidewalk—lock, stock, and barrel. There wasn't a moving van in sight, only rain clouds.

The major **credit information providers** are TransUnion, Experian, and Equifax. In accordance with the federal Fair Credit Reporting Act, all such industry companies are required to provide their particular version to you (see the URLs at the end of this chapter). For that, they charge a nominal fee, but it does include your FICO score. Examine the report for accuracy. If you find an error, the provider is obliged to correct it upon proof. You also have the right to dispute an erroneous entry.

You have the right to a free copy as well, but this one omits your FICO. Bring up the webpage listed in the Helpful Links and follow the directions to order your complimentary credit report online, by mail, or by calling a toll-free number. This is safer than searching on "free credit report." That brings up a variety of options, some of which could spell trouble. Imposter sites with similar names wait patiently to capture your Social Security number and steal your identity. In addition, the trustworthy webpage guides you in correcting reporting errors and filing a complaint. Moreover, there's important industry news and information about grants, housing, and jobs. Check it out.

The FICO score is an indicative analytic, which considers all reported information—both favorable and unfavorable—and produces a creditworthiness score, which ranges from a low of 300 to a high of 850. The system uses complex parameters which give lenders a pretty accurate picture of how you've handled debt so far and tries to predict how you'll react in the near future. But it isn't completely intuitive. For instance, financially responsible people who've never borrowed a nickel might very well score low.

Naturally, you want an attractive credit report, so let's see if we can find ways that you can help yourself as we look at how credit builds.

Reported data first begins accumulating with your first account application. This and all future credit requests are known as "inquiries." Once you've established an account with, say, an Internet service provider, that company will automatically report your payments, thereby expanding your history. Those payments can be made (in a timely fashion) with a check, money order, or online. You can also put points on the board in other ways: For merchants that don't report your purchase activity, such as gas stations and department stores, buy what you need with a credit card, and then make that payment on time. The credit card issuer will then send your activity record to the credit reporting companies, such as Experian and TransUnion. That strategy increases the number of times you've used debt responsibly, and it will then be reflected in your FICO. For those of you who can't yet qualify for a credit card, you can mimic this habit with a gift card or prepaid card. Another helpful way to raise your FICO is asking your property management company to periodically report your prompt rental payments (assuming that it works directly with a credit bureau).

To better see the scope and nature of what credit report providers collect, access the URLs at the end of this chapter. Experian, for example, illustrates a sample credit report. In addition, Trans-Union provides its Credit Report User's Guide. Both PDFs will be enlightening.

I hate to leave you, but now I can do so in the knowledge that you're better prepared to run the business of your life. Good luck to you.

Helpful Links

Consumer Credit Counseling Service

https://credit.org/cccs

Government Information on Credit Reports

https://www.usa.gov/credit-reports

Credit Reports

Experian

https://www.experian.com

https://www.experian.com/credit_report_basics/pdf/samplecreditreport.pdf

TransUnion

https://www.transunion.com

https://www.transunion.com/resources/transunion/doc/compliance-and-legislative-updates/HowToReadCreditReport.pdf

Equifax

https://www.equifax.com/personal

Federal Trade Commission on Free Credit Report

https://www.ftc.gov/faq/consumer-protection/get-my-free-credit-report

Free Annual Credit Report

https://www.annualcreditreport.com

INDEX

TEAR-OUT PAGES

Worksheet to Balance Your Account

Step A

Enter the ending balance on this statement. $ _____

Step B

In the table below, list outstanding deposits and other credits to your account that do not appear on this statement:

Description	Amount
Total	$

Table B total $ _____

Step C

Add the box total to Step A and enter at the right. $ _____

Step D

Below, list outstanding checks, withdrawals, and other debits to your account that do not appear on this statement.

Description	Amount
Total	$

Table D total $ _____

Step E

Subtract the Step D total from Step C to calculate the adjusted ending balance. This amount should be the same as the current balance shown in your register.

Budget Formulation's First Step

Fixed Expenses

_____

_____

_____

_____

_____

_____

_____

_____

Variable Expenses

_____

_____

_____

_____

_____

_____

Discretionary Expenses

_____

_____

_____

_____

_____

_____

_____

Tear-out 2   Budget Formation—Step One

Budget Formulation, Step Two

Name _____

Budget for the month of _____

Income

Wages/tips/salary $ _____

Allowance   (If you have one)   _____

Other   (Odd jobs, gifts, etc.)   _____

Total Income $ _____

Expenses

Fixed (in order of importance)

_____ $ _____

_____   _____

_____   _____

Variable (in order of importance)

_____ $ _____

_____   _____

_____   _____

_____   _____

Discretionary (most common to least)

_____   _____

_____   _____

_____   _____

_____   _____

Total Expenses $ _____

Unspent Money $ _____
(Subtract your totals, and there you have it.)

Tear-out 3   Budget Formation—Step Two

Budget Forecast Worksheet

	January Forecast	Actual Results	Difference	February Forecast	Actual Results	Difference	March Forecast	Actual Results	Difference
Income									
Take-home pay	$	$	$	$	$	$	$	$	$
Monthly Allowance									
Miscellaneous									
Cash flow carryover (C)									
Total (A)									
Expenses									
	$	$	$	$	$	$	$	$	$
Total (B)	$	$	$	$	$	$	$	$	$
Cash Flow Analysis									
Income total (A)	$	$	$	$	$	$	$	$	$
Subtract Expense total (B)									
Net income (loss) moves up to the carryover line (C) for next month	$	$	$	$	$	$	$	$	$

Tear-out 4   Budget Forecast Worksheet